Praise for *F*cked*

"Corinne and Krystyna know more about fucking than I do—and I know *everything* about fucking. Buy this book, fuckers!"

    —DAN SAVAGE, author, sex columnist, and host of *Savage Lovecast*

"Sex is so much more than the missionary position. *F*cked* is necessary literature for the people of tomorrow. Read this book, open your mind, and feel shame no more."

    —AMBER ROSE, activist, author, model, entrepreneur, and pop culture maven

"Corinne and Krystyna do the most brilliant, honest, and smart anti slut-shaming stuff. For their legions of fans, they do much more than entertain: they really help. They are great, and so is this book."

    —JON RONSON, documentary filmmaker and *New York Times* bestselling author of *So You've Been Publicly Shamed*

"Loved it. Whether you're a nice Irish boy (like myself) or a lowlife pervert (like myself) or some combination, this book will help you get real (and like yourself)."

    —COLIN QUINN, comedian and author

"I smell a hit!"

    —DAVE ATTELL, comedian, actor, and writer

"This book is for things the world has never been able to watch: a woman getting sworn in as the president of the United States, women being treated equally to men in the workplace, and the WNBA."

    —ARTIE LANGE, comedian, formerly of *The Howard Stern Show*

"These ladies parlayed talking about sex into writing about sex. I don't understand why. Writing seems like way more work. I haven't been on the podcast because I tried to hook up with Krystyna years back, and it didn't go smoothly. So, check out the book, I guess."

    —HANNIBAL BURESS, comedian and actor

"Comedians Corinne Fisher and Krystina Hutchinson delve into sex, love, and relationships in *F*cked: Being Sexually Explorative and Self-Confident in a World That's Screwed*. Like their podcast, *Guys We Fucked: The Anti Slut-Shaming Podcast*, *F*cked* takes a hilarious, no-nonsense approach. This is the book you need if you're looking for guidance on butt stuff, relationship faux pas, dealing with shaming, and much more."

—Bustle

"Mixing dating advice with stories from their own sexcapades, comedians Fisher and Hutchinson expand on themes from their popular podcast in this unabashedly blunt guide to sex. . . . [T]heir main message that women should not be ashamed of their sexuality comes across loud and clear."

—Publishers Weekly

"What sets Fisher and Hutchinson apart is their frank and funny approach to taboo topics, and they brought this same attitude to *F*cked*. The book is part manual, part confessional, and part stand-up comedy. But it is all honest as fuck."

—BUST magazine

"The book is their raw, arousing podcast put to paper, giving readers a mix of side-splitting and serious pillow talk."

—Interview Magazine

F*CKED

F*CKED

Being Sexually Explorative and Self-Confident in a World That's Screwed

Corinne Fisher & Krystyna Hutchinson

HOSTS OF *GUYS WE FUCKED: THE ANTI SLUT-SHAMING PODCAST*

HarperOne
An Imprint of HarperCollinsPublishers

HarperOne

The names and identifying characteristics of some of the individuals featured throughout this book have been changed to protect their privacy.

This book is coauthored by Corinne Fisher and Krystyna Hutchinson. The author of each chapter is identified at the beginning of each section, excluding "Quoth the Boyfriend, 'Nevermore'," "Why We're Fucked," "Historical Roots," and "Religion," which were written by Corinne Fisher, and "But First, a Message from Our Listeners," which was written by Krystyna Hutchinson.

HarperCollins books may be purchased for educational, business, or sales promotional use. For information, please email the Special Markets Department at SPsales@harpercollins.com.

FIRST HARPERCOLLINS PAPERBACK EDITION PUBLISHED IN 2019

Designed by Kris Tobiassen of Matchbook Digital

Illustrations by Elise Perry

Library of Congress Cataloging-in-Publication Data is available upon request.

ISBN 978-0-06-266692-5

19 20 21 22 23   LSC   10 9 8 7 6 5 4 3 2 1

For the women who were strong and feminist when it was both in and out of fashion: Marcia Clark, Hillary Clinton, the Spice Girls, and, of course, my mom.

—CORINNE

For my parents, who taught me to dream big, work hard, and laugh at all the bullshit. For my BFF, Melissa. And for all the Fuckers.

—KRYSTYNA

Contents

RELATIONSHIPS

SAFE SEX AND SERIOUS STUFF

CONCLUSION

INTRODUCTION

Quoth the Boyfriend, "Nevermore"

Are you a degenerate cum dumpster who isn't worthy of love or affection? Probably not, but odds are someone has made you feel that way at one point in time.

Hi! We're Corinne Fisher and Krystyna Hutchinson, cohosts of *Guys We Fucked: The Anti Slut-Shaming Podcast,* a weekly comedic discussion about human sexuality, relationships, and taboos that has garnered an absurdly large and loyal following (mostly because people feel a greater sense of sexual shame and hookup hang-ups than we could have ever imagined).

The catalyst for the podcast went down inside a Panera Bread with Corinne and her boyfriend at the time—a man who will be referred to from this point on as 'Panera.' After she purchased her broke, also-a-comic beau of two years a You Pick Two combo, complete with the ninety-nine-cent dessert add-on, he told her, "I can't do this anymore." It was a breakup breakdown of epic proportions, partly because Corinne had just lost the love of her life and partly because she realized how much control she had allowed a man to have over her happiness for so long. She spent months thinking about this, mostly using comedy as rehab, and began interrogating everyone she knew about their boyfriends, girlfriends, marriages, and breakups. She was on her way to becoming the Barbara Walters of relationships.

After almost a year of reflection, including drawing way too much of a correlation between the Katy Perry–Russell Brand breakup and her own, Corinne got an idea. An awful idea. Corinne got a wonderful, *awful* idea. Influenced perhaps a little too much by movies starring John Cusack, she decided to take a cue from *High Fidelity* and go back and interview every boyfriend and sex partner she'd ever had to figure out what she was doing wrong. But for an undertaking of this level, one needs a friend, so Corinne sent a text to her longtime comedy partner, Krystyna, the other half of the Sorry About Last Night . . . duo. The two girls had already made somewhat of a splash on the local comedy scene with their BYOB variety shows, rap music videos dedicated to shitty roommates, recaps of the show *Girls,* and self-titled two-woman show at the Upright Citizens Brigade Theatre in Chelsea, so to pair up on this new venture seemed only natural.

From its inception at a dining room table at 151 Kent Ave. in Williamsburg, Brooklyn, the goal of Sorry About Last Night . . . had always been to create comedy with a purpose, and this idea seemed to capture that notion quite succinctly. By sitting down with people from our past, we would become our best selves for the future. After a few whiskey-infused meetings, including one in which Krystyna

suggested adding "The Anti Slut-Shaming Podcast" to the show's title, we pitched our idea to Stand Up NY Labs, the original home of *Guys We Fucked*, who accepted our edgy concept with open arms.

Corinne knew exactly who she wanted to start with for the first episode: Vinnie Vitale, a charming, handsome—albeit neurotic—comedian from Vernon, New Jersey, who had been her on-again, off-again fling post-Panera. He adored Corinne, and she adored that adoration. After propositioning Vinnie one final time, this one being nonsexual and in a Coffee Bean at the corner of Bleecker and Macdougal, their fate was sealed.

The episode, ultimately entitled "Vinnie: Can I Choke You?" started with Corinne recounting her recent (and only) one-night stand with another Jersey boy, Anthony from Atlantic City, and Krystyna complaining about getting mistaken for a stripper. It ended up being listened to by over five hundred thousand people. Listeners seemed to immediately gravitate toward our open and honest approach to sexuality, because, they said, it made them feel like they were hanging out with their friends. As the interviews with former flings, fuck buddies, and ex-boyfriends piled up, so did the e-mails in our inbox. Without prodding, subscribers began to furiously seek sex, dating, and relationship advice from us—two pretty regular twenty-somethings. And all those e-mails were connected by one overbearing common thread: *shame*.

These letters from strangers served as an alarming wake-up call about society's relationship with sexuality. So we began to dive deeper with our guests and our subject matter—the darker, the better. While comedy was still the glue that held every fucked up story together, we regularly laughed *and* cried with our guests about abortion, pedophilia, rape, sexual assault, domestic abuse, stalking, and suicide.

What started out as a self-centered endeavor to explore more about ourselves quickly morphed into something bigger. Doing our podcast has taught us how necessary it is to have women be confident and vocal about their sexual choices, be shameless but smart about them, and be serious but with a sense of humor (something sorely lacking in both sexuality and feminism). We are those women. The only shame we would ever feel is if we didn't write this book.

After reading three years' worth of e-mails from strangers of every age, gender, race, and sexual orientation, and from all around the world, the one thing we can say for certain is that whatever flavor of sexual shame you may have, you are not alone. While this book won't be able to magically heal you, it may allow you to see yourself in a different way. If you're struggling to get over a breakup, coping with sexual trauma, or just dealing with the awkwardness of being human, we hope reading this will allow the healing process to continue, or begin. Self-help is not selfish. In fact, we believe it's the most selfless thing you can do. By taking time to better yourself, you will be a better partner. If the airplane of your life is going down, you have to properly affix your oxygen mask before helping anyone else. We know this because we've seen it with our podcast guests, in e-mails from our listeners, and in our own lives. While we're not necessarily suggesting you air your sexual laundry for the entire world to hear (that's kind of our thing), we can certainly say the lessons from our podcast are universal, and transformative.

Perhaps the biggest transformation has been in how the two of us understand ourselves. We've left no taboo stone unturned, and our conversations have frequently highlighted the delightful differences between us. The topics, while oft polarizing, have done us the great service of showcasing our *Odd Couple* juxtaposition of personalities. Corinne, three years older and a resident of New York City since age seventeen, is aggressively realistic, open-minded, sarcastic, wise, and food driven, while Krystyna is loquacious, optimistic, curious, kindhearted, and a proud member of the Church of Beyoncé. If you already listen to the podcast, you know this. If you don't, prepare to meet your hosts.

Corinne

Self-esteem isn't everything.
It's just that there's nothing without it.

—Gloria Steinem

I've always had a gift for making people laugh. The first time I remember really "going for it" is in Mrs. Swanson's kindergarten class. Mrs. Swanson had left the classroom for reasons unknown (I'm hoping a tawdry affair, but I don't want to start rumors), which to young Corinne was the equivalent of putting a staircase in front of a Broadway stage with a sign that says OPEN CALL. I knew I needed a quick bit, nothing too wordy or clever that would go over the heads of these plebeians I was forced to learn the alphabet with. I needed a crowd-pleaser. Perhaps an act-out? I channeled Dane Cook before I even knew who he was, lifted the half shirt given to me by my Jewish grandmother (who thought until her dying day that nudity was the biggest sin), and revealed my nubile areolas. Some of my classmates cackled, some were shocked into silence by the avant-garde nature of my performance, and of course one future I'd-like-to-speak-to-the-manager bitch squealed on me. Ugh, women. We continually hold one another back. Good thing I was smart enough to woman her right back, bat my eyelashes at the teacher, and charm my way out of any possible trouble. Apparently, when you have a squeaky clean track record, you get to lift your top now and again without repercussions. And that's the best reason for staying in line anyone will ever give you.

With my first impromptu solo performance securely under the elastic waistband of my culottes, I realized I was a content creator and could no longer be held down by the silent shackles of beach blanket naptime. I would use every opportunity from that moment on to shake things up a bit. And for a very long time I was my own talent manager, fan club president, and publicist. Channeling my inner Lucy Ricardo for the next twenty years or so, I continually tried to metaphorically convince Ricky to let me perform at Club Babalu.

When at the age of almost twenty-seven I was dumped by the aforementioned ex-boyfriend in the aforementioned Panera Bread, for a second (okay, more like a year) I lost the shine that had brought my kindergarten class to a halt. I spent almost every night in comedy clubs exchanging relationship war stories with fellow comics and turning my pain into punchlines. I hadn't been single for more than six months since I'd turned eighteen, but during that year I took a honeymoon with my adult self. It wasn't just a romantic staycation for one. It was also a wake-up call about women, including myself. There was no question in my mind that the female comics I worked with every night were strong, self-sufficient people—you have to be to exist in this business—but I came to the jarring realization that a huge percentage of almost every one of our sets was about men and the sex, relationships, and troubles we have with them. Even though we had proven ourselves worthy of equal stage time, we were still letting men steal our spotlight by making a lot of our material about them. We were allowing the men in our lives to determine our value and overshadow all the other things we had to offer audiences apart from our relationship status. And so, after standing by as we all sold ourselves short night and night again, I along with Katie Hannigan, fellow comic and one of my favorite friends, took on a challenge: spend three months writing and workshopping twenty minutes of material not about men, sex, or relationships, and present it to the city of New York in something we would call *The Comedienne Project*. After the healing that came in the form of the *Guys We Fucked* podcast, this was my second very public act of self-love, but it was the first public act to acknowledge head-on that loving yourself doesn't always mean you have to also find a partner. Sometimes loving yourself is precisely enough.

Until I began recording the *Guys We Fucked* podcast, I really had no idea just how bad people felt about themselves. As I like to bring up often, because I think it's one of her greatest comedic quotes, my mom has told me on more than one occasion that I have "*too much self-confidence*." What can I say? I've always thought I was fly as fuck before "fly as fuck" was even something people said. As a teenager, I would spend hours just admiring myself in the mirror—not my makeup or my clothing, my actual naked figure. I loved everything: my itty-bitty titties; my thick, milky thighs; my flat-enough tummy; my interesting nose with the ball on the end of it (shout-out to Sarah Michelle Gellar), and even my outie vagina, which I would learn over a decade later isn't society's preferred type. Sorry, what's that, society? I can't hear you over my screaming orgasm.

During the past almost four years of recording the podcast I've realized how rare loving yourself is, how differently I see and experience the world because I do love myself, and that the nicest gift I can give others is the ability to love themselves. I have learned a lot in the past thirty-one years of walking to the beat of my own drum. I want to help you find your own drum and your own beat. And if nothing I say helps you, maybe just put Des'ree's "You Gotta Be" on a Spotify loop and go on with your day.

I've also realized that perhaps my constant love and acceptance of my own voice and reflection, sometimes interpreted by my mother as narcissism, was really all her fault to begin with. She and my father raised my brother and I in a house where getting straight A's was our responsibility, not an option; makeup application wasn't done (and, in fact—with the exception of baton-twirling recitals and school plays—was sometimes mocked); giving back to the community through volunteer work happened long before it was needed to pad our college applications; and following the crowd was something only fools did. I had a really nice childhood, honestly, so it's really pretty amazing I still ended up messy enough to become a stand-up comedian.

I wanted to talk about being a comedian in this sex, relationship, and feminism book because it's not just an important *part* of who I am; it's who I am fully. Sure, I have other roles—daughter, girlfriend, sister, friend, woman—but comic is the role I have connected with on the deepest level. Apart from the breakup, I have rarely felt lost in my life, but I have and do often feel misunderstood and spiritually homeless—I don't quite fit in anywhere. When I started doing stand-up comedy, all the pieces suddenly clicked, the Operation table stopped making that horrific buzzing sound, and finally I felt like I had found that "purpose" I had read about in Paulo Coelho's *The Alchemist*.

I love writing. With the publishing of this book, I am adding author to the list of roles I've taken on or have had thrust upon me, which works out well because I hate talking and I love writing.

I was the weirdo in high school who hid during sports that involved running bases but would get excited when we were assigned a paper. In class, I never really cared if people thought I was nice or pretty or friendly, but I always wanted them to be moved by my writing—even if it made them mad. I've gotten in trouble a lot over the years for writing about things people didn't want me writing about. In fact, I was sent to the principal's office only one time during my four years in high school and it was for writing—an "exposé" on the Union Fire Department and how they were trying to shut down our school play (LOL). I wrote a letter to the vice principal of that same high school when an upperclassman informed me that same-sex couples were required to get a parent's signature before buying prom tickets, while straight couples did not need that same approval (and I kept pressing the issue until I was assured it wasn't so). I wrote a letter to David Sedaris when for my senior film thesis at SVA I was researching the allure folks find in keeping the secret of Santa Claus alive (he wrote back). I've written love letters, letters to my future self, letters to the editor, and letters to the daughter I'll probably never get around to having. For better or for worse, I've become my own therapist over the years through writing. I've written my way out of heartbreak, out of loss, out of disappointment. When I'm stuck or unsure, I often just write until I find an answer. I haven't found all of them yet, so I'll probably keep writing.

My love of writing comes from my mom. She's a proper English teacher these days, but she's always been a writer and has always encouraged her children to write because it gives everyone, no matter your age or your class, an outlet and a voice.

When I did something wrong, my mom sent me to my room and said, "Write about it."

When I felt disturbed or slighted by another human, my mom said, "Write to them."

When I wanted something, my mom said, "Write and ask for it."

In my hometown, there is a school called Central Five, where all the fifth graders from all the elementary schools get the opportunity to spend a year together. I got wind that some classes in this school were part of an archaeology program in which the students went to actual archaeology sites and got to excavate artifacts. I wanted to be in one of the classes that did this more than anything, so my mom told me I should write a letter to the principal. I wrote that letter, and while the principal never formally wrote me back, out of all the classes I could've been placed in, I was put in one that was part of that archaeology program. I knew it was because I had written that letter, and it made me feel powerful, in control of my own destiny.

My teacher that year was a curly-haired woman named Mrs. Bundy, who signed my yearbook with a message that I think of often: "When you write a book, I would like the first signed copy." I promised to send it to her. Twenty-one years later, I can finally make good on that promise. So I guess what I'm trying to say is that I wrote a book and I couldn't be more fucking excited. Well, kind of. I wrote half a book, but I'm hoping Mrs. Bundy will still appreciate the gesture.

 ## A Word from the Woman Who Made Corinne (aka Corinne's Mom)

I can't take credit for raising Corinne with some grand plan to instill confidence, but I did contribute good genes. I come from a line of confident women. My maternal grandmother, Alice, a true character, married two weeks before the 1929 stock market crash that started the Great Depression, and she raised her family during World War II. In her sixties, Grandma decided to see the world, so she and her sister, my great-aunt Helen, embarked on a series of cruises to the great cities of Europe. I'm a baby boomer who grew up in a typical suburban tract house, but even as a child I understood that the equal partnership of my parents' marriage defied that era's norm. My mother and father made decisions together, each respecting the thoughts and feelings of the other, which reflected a quiet yet potent strength. A smart kid, I excelled in school and, before girl power was a thing, relished beating a boy for top academic honors at my eighth-grade graduation. During Corinne's childhood I was a stay-at-home mom, but when she reached high school, I earned my master's in education and became a teacher, showing her that learning and growing is a lifelong process.

Unsurprisingly, Corinne has always had a strong sense of self, the hallmark of confidence. My earliest realization that Corinne could not be easily cowed occurred when she was in kindergarten. After school one day, she relayed the story of how she'd had quite enough of her classmate Dylan's comments about her "nice legs" and had told him in no uncertain terms, "Cut. It. Out." When the Boys & Girls Club dances began in fifth grade, girls who sat on the bleachers waiting for a boy to ask them to dance exasperated her. In seventh grade, during a school trip, the popular clique (which Corinne later dubbed the "snob mob") was planning to go epic "mean girl" on Corinne throughout the excursion. When Corinne discovered the plot, she managed to change accommodations to room with Paula and Kelly, who then became her very best friends on through high school graduation. (As podcast listeners know, Paula remains Corinne's BFF to this very day.) In the ultimate middle school power move, Corinne, Paula, and Kelly returned home from the trip wearing matching shirts they had bought as souvenirs.

I often wish I could bottle Corinne's self-assurance to give to those teenagers and young adults who are so uncomfortable in their own skin, but even that wouldn't be enough, because problems with confidence extend beyond adolescence. Peer and societal pressures can corrode a person's self-esteem at any age. As a result, too many people spend their lives trying to become the person they think the world is telling them to be rather than the person they really are. Losing the need for approval from others is liberating. Best of all, it provides the freedom to take the very risks that bring life's greatest rewards.

Corinne has always been a force of nature, and I suspect she always will be. After all, she was born in the wake of Hurricane Gloria. As an English major, I should have recognized the foreshadowing. ■

Krystyna

Independence comes from knowing who you are
and you being happy with yourself.
—Beyoncé

Not only has my glass always been half-full, it's straight-up overflowing onto the floor. I'm the type of optimist who naively overestimates what I'm capable of. I was lucky enough to be raised by two parents I love and respect beyond words. My mother is a beautiful soul of a woman, and the strength and grace she was forced to have in order to deal with a laundry list of mental and physical health obstacles has inspired me to power through whatever life throws my way. I tend to have dramatic reactions to small problems more often than I'd like to admit, but I always think of what she has to go through on a daily basis and I realize that I'm being a shithead. I credit my mother for my endless supply of empathy and self-awareness. She claims that I wasn't a huge bitch to her during my teenage years, but I have vivid memories of screaming at her because she wouldn't let my sixteen-year-old ass drive two hours on a highway, by myself, to visit my college-aged boyfriend, whom she knew was no good (she was right). *"Why do you freaking hate me, Mom? Do you not want me to be happy?!"* Most of my arguments with her were boy related.

One of our biggest arguments occurred after I admitted to her, a few months after the fact, that I had lost my virginity at the age of sixteen. We were at a restaurant when I told her, and I'll never forget the look of disappointment on her face when the words left my mouth. She walked out of the restaurant and was beside herself for weeks. I always got agonizingly uncomfortable whenever the subject of sex was brought up in front of my parents. To this day, if I'm watching a movie with them and a sex scene comes on, panic sets in and I'm like "Oh! Gotta pee! Drinking so much water today, ha-ha! Okay, bye!" and I get the hell out of that room.

My father has been my emotional rock and kept me sane all throughout my life. Despite his seemingly unemotional demeanor, he's a giant teddy bear of a man who has taught me the values of hard work, personal responsibility, and how important it is to vote. The only thing I hate about getting older is watching him not be able to physically do all the bad-ass, athletic, cool shit he used to. My dad was a chief in the United States Navy and retired with an E8 rank after spending years on aircraft carriers, repairing jet plane engines and traveling the world. This earned him many accolades, including being honored by the president. He has since developed diabetes and could theoretically die from eating too many cupcakes. Regardless, he is my hero.

The glue that has successfully held my parents' relationship together for thirty-eight years is laughter. My dad's sarcastic sense of humor paired with my mother's whimsical ingenuity is a large part of who I am as a woman and a comedian, and I feel fortunate every day that Nancy and Edward are my parents. Their love, support, and sense of humor gave me self-assurance and a bright outlook on life. So much so that I pursued a career in comedy.

That said (you knew there had to be a "but"), when your glass is always overflowing with joy, love, and rainbows, it tends to cloud your judgment. For better or worse (usually worse), I always see the best in people, even if I have to squint my eyes really hard to get through all the mess. If there is a laundry list of shitty qualities about you, you bet your ass I will find your three best traits and focus only on those for as long as I can until time forces your intolerable true colors to surface. I am a narcissist's dream girl!

This has made dating somewhat of a roller coaster for me. Fortunately, for the past six years I have been in the kind of romantic relationship I thought existed only in movies, with a man by the name of Stephen. I love him more than any poem or card or song could ever articulate. Whenever I think about how much he means to me, I tear the fuck up. I'm doing it right now! I've never met anyone quite like Stephen. He has taught me how to effectively communicate how I feel and ask for what I want emotionally and sexually, which has opened my eyes to what a romantic relationship can be. More on Stephen later!

When I look back at the arc of my sexuality, I always laugh. Starting at the age of six or seven, I was humping anything and everything in my house. It all started with a giant stuffed horse that "Santa" got me one year for Christmas—a tale as old as time. I wouldn't do it in front of people because for some reason I understood that masturbation was a private activity, but the second I was alone: Hump City, bitch. Sure, I was low-key horrified that masturbating somehow meant that I could become pregnant at any moment, but I managed to shove that fear under the rug in exchange for physical pleasure. Alas, this knowledge of how to make myself orgasm did not carry over into partnered sex until much later in life. I've heard stories from my straight guy friends about the first time they saw a pair of boobs or a lady's butt in their mom's JCPenney bra catalog when they were kids. That life-altering moment of discovery they describe sounds so thrilling! I never had that as a kid. I wasn't hanging out in my room, going "What's a girl gotta do to get a glimpse of some dicks around here?!" The stuffed animal horse did the job just fine, and—bonus—it didn't look like a one-eyed snake monster.

My sex life has evolved from trying to hide being in physical pain with my very first boyfriend and feeling betrayed over him watching porn to frequenting strip clubs, sex clubs, sex toy stores, and having threesomes with Stephen. I've come a long way since being emotionally scarred and stunted by, of all things, my boobs.

Nothing could prepare me for the day I developed breasts. It broke my heart. Shopping for a bra with my mom was a symbol of losing my childhood. I remember the woman in the department store trying to help me find a bra that I'd like while at the same time assuring me that bras did not symbolize the loss of innocence. Boy, was that lady wrong. I begged my mom to let me get sports bras, and they both laughed at me. "Aw, come on, you don't want to make them smaller!" the lady said. Ha! She was half-correct. I didn't want to make them smaller, I wanted to cut them off my body and throw them in the dumpster behind the mall.

As you may have guessed, or if you've heard me bitch about it on the podcast, it only got worse from there. By the time I was in ninth grade, I was a 32DD. Grown men would sexualize me, and a select few of my female classmates would accuse me of sticking my chest out to get the attention of boys. Unfortunately, I didn't have the wherewithal to tell those people to fuck off (or even a nice version of "Fuck off"). Instead, I internalized everyone's negative attention toward my body and hid my boobs from the world. Or at least I tried. As Corinne often says to me, "Krystyna, if you put a sheet over a giant television, you can still tell there's a giant television underneath it." Ugh. So true.

In the beginning of high school, my nickname was Big D's McGee, and even though I laughed it off, it made me want to retreat further into my shell. Being sexualized because of how you look on the outside, when you still feel like a joyful, Barbie-loving, innocent little girl on the inside, *blows*. It made me realize that life can be cruel. As a person who is allergic to sadness, that traumatized me a bit. I rarely wear low-cut shirts, and I'm angered that I have absorbed other people's opinions so much. Yet when I do decide to show some cleavage, it confirms for me that I'm not the kind of person who can emotionally handle it, as trivial as that may sound. It takes me back to being fourteen years old and wearing my backpack in the front so the construction worker or the creepy neighbor or the shit bag driving by in his car wouldn't feel the need to voice his opinion on how much he enjoyed my curves.

Thankfully, the older I get, the more I realize that the only person's opinion you should ever be concerned with is your own. Once you truly understand that and live by it, the world is your oyster. Since achieving moderate Internet fame, Corinne and I have had some gnarly shit said about us. One sad man wrote an entire article about the podcast, calling Corinne and I fun things like "pathetic cum dumpsters" and "fat sluts." My favorite part was when he assumed our fathers either left us when we were babies or were too ashamed to speak to us anymore. This may come as a shock to some folks, but when I look at myself in the mirror, I don't see a pathetic cum dumpster or a fat, fatherless slut. I see a fun bitch with a great rack and a heart of gold.

This Book

Within the first six months of recording *Guys We Fucked,* we were offered our first book deal by an editor who had published the sideways sexploits of a comedian we love and admire. While we were thrilled at the prospect, he quickly began pressuring us to alter our nonfiction sex stories into tawdry supermarket checkout tales with long descriptions of dick size that made fun of how stupid the men we fucked had been. But that wasn't our style and certainly wasn't the case, so we passed. We were tired of these books that pander to women like we're all hot messes, unable to handle our emotions without the assistance of a man, a glass of rosé, and a Xanax. This book is the antidote to all that noise. It will show the reader—be you male, female, transgender, or undecided—that you deal with shit, you brush your shoulder off like Jay-Z, and you move the fuck on. In a society where for some reason it has become chic to be the victim, we say this pity party ends now.

This manual won't be just for dames post-breakup and couples thinking of having a threesome. We're going to deal with the darker topics that most sexual self-help books won't cover. We'll go right from butt stuff to abortions, from sexual harassment to body shaming, because the overly cautious dialogue about these topics thus far has been hindering the cause. This book will take over where your therapist left off, because we wholeheartedly believe that the best way to feel better isn't for someone else to guide you through your feelings, it's to be strong enough to have the ability to laugh yourself through the pain. This is more than a book about how to step away from the Ben & Jerry's if Jeff won't text you back. This is a book that will help you to be a person who would never let Jeff have enough power over you to open that pint to begin with (unless you just want a snack, then that's fine).

A lot of books are by "experts" so sure of what you should do that they're willing to make you feel terrible if you don't follow their instructions to a T. Well, we can't tell you what to do because that's your job. We do, however, have a laundry list of things we would suggest not doing based on our own experiences. This is a what-not-to-do manual, if you will. Based on true events, of course.

This is a guide to love and sex for women who drink whiskey because they like it, not because it's a cute thing to say on your Tinder profile. It has no trigger warnings, because life doesn't come with those. It won't talk down to you or hold you while you're crying. You're not weak. You can get through this. We're not going to explain to you why he's just not that into you, because it doesn't fucking matter. Despite what television, rom-coms, and glossy beauty mags tell you, you're fine all by yourself. This is the book Bridget Jones should've read instead of writing that shitty diary in the first place.

Self-help guides are kind of bullshit because, well, if they really worked, we'd all be smiling, journaling, and juicing 24/7. We all from time to time have a tumultuous relationship with our sexuality—think of this book as a mental detox from the crap you've been fed regarding the choices you've made with your body. Sex isn't evil, and talking about it is the first step in your personal erotic exorcism. So let's talk about fuckin'!

But First, a Message from Our Listeners

We never asked the listeners of our podcast to e-mail us seeking advice. We were still trying to figure out our own lives by word-vomiting into a microphone every week and telling the Internet all about our sex-capades. For whatever reason, this prompted a few folks to write in, asking for our opinions on their problems. When we started reading the e-mails on air, they began to pour into our inbox by the hundreds. It was shocking to discover how many people in this world are going through some serious shit. We get everything from "Is it okay to fuck when the dog is in the room?" to "How can I stop hating my nipples?" We love our inbox. It's a treasure chest of sexual secrets from people of all ages, races, genders, and sexual orientations. It's made us realize that we humans have a lot in common. And the simple act of talking about all our baggage can change someone's life. These e-mails have also opened our eyes to serious problems in our culture—problems that happen to *way* more people than you may realize and that are often rooted in low self-worth and a deep sense of shame. Whether it's an insecurity about your boyfriend's porn habit, a fear about your lack of libido, or embarrassment about your pepperoni nipples, you can pretty much trace the roots of each dilemma back to an underlying belief that you are wrong for wanting what you want, gross for looking how you look, and in general, a certified weirdo. To demonstrate this, we thought we'd give you a glimpse of our box. Our *inbox*, you perv.

Without further ado, here is just a teeny-weeny sampling of letters we've received in the SALN mailbox re: "shame"!

....

To: SorryAboutLastNightShow@gmail.com
Sent: Friday, November 11, 2016, 11:40 P.M.
Subject: Should there be shame in my 1 child game?

I'm obviously a fan because I'm emailing you some semi personal shit that I would like your opinion on. I live in Utah, lots and lots of Mormons which means big families! My in laws are all Mormons and have many children. (They are great and I love them, not trying to bad mouth here.) We are a little different because my husband and I have only 1 child and both want to keep it that way. This brings some confusion and judgment, I feel, from his family. They ask us all the time if we are going to have more, our answer is always the same, "probably not." I don't think we need to explain ourselves and our situation but my husband usually gives a detailed answer. Here's a little of our history.

We got married, got pregnant, had a little girl (who is the coolest/ best human being) but I had severe postpartum depression. I suffered with it for a little under 2 years until I finally sought professional help. All the time I just thought something was wrong with me and to be honest I was extremely embarrassed about having these problems. I was numb. Each day I put on a happy face but deep down I wanted so desperately to fall asleep and never wake up again. Depression is so horrible, it literally took over my world. Now I am finally happy and healthy again and no longer have these feelings (I'm on a great anti-depressant that works very well for me.) Anyway I confided in his family and told them this. They are very sympathetic and feel bad I had to go through this alone, which I appreciate. When they ask why we don't want any more children, my husband reminds them of the postpartum and explains it will most likely come with another child and we can't go through that again. But really to us, we have no desire to have another baby, we never get baby hungry and I honestly love the little trio we have going on! This is my happy, and I'm very grateful for my husband and daughter; that being said, what I want is us, just us. Of course we worry in my daughter's perspective of how this could affect her. I don't like thinking of her growing up alone but I don't think I should have another child just to be her "friend." Am I selfish? Yeah, maybe. But we are young so who knows what will happen in the future, but for now it's just not up for question. The shitty thing is I know there is judgement and talk about this situation because my sisters-in-law have on numerous occasions said backhanded remarks like, "this is only child syndrome" "she gets what she wants" "she needs a friend" they LOVE to point this out when she acts up. But give her a fucking break she is 3, I personally don't know any 3-year-olds who like to share, not saying they're not out there, but come on. What do you think? I'm glad that this is a tiny problem we have and I realize there are many more urgent emails that you need to respond to. I respect your opinions and hope to know what you think I should do in this situation. Anything? Nothing? Not sure why it bothers me so but it does! And I don't want to resent people who I truly love and care for, but at this point I just want people to stop criticizing my daughter and realize this is what we think is best for the three of us. For now at least.

I'm sure I'll be emailing you again, thanks for the humor!
Xox, Lady with 1 baby

To: SorryAboutLastNightShow@gmail.com
Sent: Monday, March 28, 2016, 11:46 P.M.
Subject: thank you queens

To My Queens,

At 20 years old, I've found that the past few years of navigating
my entrance into adulthood have been difficult (as I'm sure it
is for everyone). There's been the normal growing up shit, like
family drama, and then there's been the not so normal shit that
blindsides you. I've been raped twice. I hate even writing that . . .
it feels dramatic. I was 18 and had just moved to the area the
first time I was raped, and I was almost 20 the second time. I
say that it feels dramatic for a couple reasons: 1) being raped
once is sad and devastating, but twice is embarrassing and
feels like overkill, and 2) even as a victim of rape, it feels like I'm
undeserving of that title because the rapes were not violent. I
know that's ridiculous to say, because I understand the definition
of rape and that it can be both violent and nonviolent, and I'm a
proud fucking feminist who knows that despite nonviolent rape,
they were still NOT ENTITLED TO MY BODY. The irony of this
is that being raped caused my feminist awakening. Feminism
found me soon after the first time, when I was feeling broken
and disgusting. I blamed myself, and I was in a cloud of denial,
despite the rational things the doctors told me happened to my
body, despite the memory of a pill being shoved in my mouth,
despite waking up naked with no recollection of anything after
that pill, and despite bleeding from my vagina for a week.
Somehow, I ignored it all, even though "rape" couldn't have
been spelled out any more clearly. The only thing that made me
feel better in the weeks and months after being so grossly taken

advantage of was when I typed "rape" into the search bar of Tumblr (I don't have Tumblr, but the Tumblr world seemed warm and welcoming and a good place to search the term "rape"). Upon searching, I was greeted with so many memes about women's rights and the fundamental concept that men are not ever fucking entitled to our bodies. It was through my Tumblr browsing that I realized what happened to me was not my fault; it should not have happened and I was in no damn way "asking for it." Discovering feminism and readily agreeing with the concept on a core level is what helped me cross the bridge from denial to anger in being raped. Unfortunately, there are plenty of gross men out there who are horrible and feel entitled to getting their dick wet, and I was raped again after feeling emotionally stable and healed from what had happened before. This time was at a party on the island where I worked and I got really drunk (cause I'm a human and I'm allowed to get drunk if I damn well please, @thepatriarchy), and a guy who I worked with took advantage of my passed out, absolutely fucking wasted self on a couch. The only thing I remember from that night is the beginning when I started drinking, and later on waking up seeing him on top of me and inside of me, and passing out again after. The next morning, after examining bruises on my body (from falling drunk) and trying to piece together the night, I remembered that guy on top of me and just started bawling, asking my friend and coworker "How the *fuck* does this happen twice to someone? Am I just an easy target?"

It's been about seven months since that island party, and I've grown into an even stronger woman than I was before. Some of that is from putting all of my energy into my goals and being good to myself, and some of that is from exceptional women who inspire me, like you two. Discovering your podcast was such a blessing. I love you guys and all the stuff you talk about, from the surface-level shit that makes me laugh out loud and bow down to you as Comedy Queens, to the deep shit that gives me all of the feels and makes me want to hug you both when I'm not even a hugger. Thanks for setting a precedent to both women and men on what a healthy and progressive mentality of sex looks like. Thanks for what you guys do. It's important.

....

To: SorryAboutLastNightShow@gmail.com
Sent: Friday, August 5, 2016, 3:58 P.M.
Subject: I'm scared I will become a pedophile, or that I already am one.

Hey guys,

I want to preface this story by saying that I have grown up in a household with two women as my parental figures (my mother and my grandmother), and my father has been absent for most of my life. I am 19 years old, a junior in college and an openly gay man. The lack of a father figure in my life has caused me to [choose] older men for sexual partners, and in the past 10 years, I have been sexually assaulted on multiple occasions. The first assault occurred at age 10 when a nephew of one of my cousins groped my groin while we were at my cousin's house. The next (and final) few assaults occurred at age 15 when I was seduced by my (same) cousin's husband, who was nearly 40. This time the sexual acts were consensual, but as you obviously know, I couldn't actually give consent because I was so young. It was about this time last year that I came to the realization that I had been a victim of statutory rape, and that fact began to weigh heavily on my psyche.

It was also around this time that I remembered an incident that occurred when I was 11 and was helping babysit at a friend of my mom's house. While my mom ran somewhere for an unknown reason, I was left at the house with our family friend's kid. It should be known that around this time I had discovered masturbation. I remember that I was told not to leave the kid I was babysitting in a room alone. I got the urge to masturbate while my mother was gone, and so I did, in full view of the kid, who was one or two at the time. I was not aroused by him whatsoever, but the fact that I allowed myself to touch myself while he was there has weighed heavily on my mind and has made me incredibly ashamed of myself. That incident, along with every incident that I suffered through, has caused me to become concerned that I might have urges to touch kids one day. I am now uncomfortable around my best friend's child, and worry that I can't trust myself to be a loving and mentally healthy father to a child one day. When I am around children, I am not aroused by them, but I can't get the image of myself hurting them in that way out of my head. I would NEVER consciously believe that sexually assaulting a child would be okay, but I am afraid that these images will never leave my head and that eventually they will evolve into something much more serious.

I have never told a single person about this. Remembering this incident causes me so much shame that I contemplate suicide on a daily to weekly basis. I don't believe I could do this to myself, but I am seriously worried about my mental health. I am currently in therapy for my issues stemming from the absence of my father, as well as the sexual assaults, depression, and anxiety. I am too scared and ashamed to tell my therapist about this out of fear of not receiving beneficial care in dealing with the issue, but I am afraid if this incident continues to go undiscussed, I will never get the help I need. It should also be noticed that while I'm a pretty sexual person, I find it very hard to allow myself to search for a relationship or casual sex, and am starting to wonder how these feelings fit into the larger picture in regards to the sexual incidents that have occurred in my life. I desperately need advice, and listening to your podcast has not only brought so much laughter and new knowledge and understanding to my life, but has brought me the courage to speak about this. If you would like to ask me any questions about this email, you are certainly encouraged to.

Thanks guys,
Scared Junior

Damn. Who knew that sex plus shame equals infinite material? We certainly didn't, but after years of discussing those two things, there's no end in sight.* We see this on tour during our live shows as well, when people literally line up to hash out their mortifying—and usually totally normal—sexual skeletons. The good news is, the more we realize that people are being shamed for the same thing, the less powerful the shame becomes.

So what's our advice? If you're being shamed about something, don't keep it to yourself. Secrecy feeds shame. When released into the open air, shame loses its power. *Own your feelings, thoughts, opinions, viewpoints, and self-worth.* To feel shame, you must relinquish ownership of those things. Which is easy if you never felt true ownership over them in the first place. But how do we lose ownership of the very things that make us who we are? Glad you asked.

---

* To illustrate this, we've included REAL subject lines from the emails we've received at the start of each section of this book. See the next page? Those are all subject lines from actual listener emails. Told you our inbox is a magical place.

condoms at my university.

hy am ashamed of
asturbating???

Fucking My Ex-Boyfriend's Dad

Parent died and so did my sex drive

nd Confidence Problem

Not knowing you're being
talked down to by a man?

How can I gain sexual confidence?

Fu
w

My sister is slut shaming me
and my friends and people she
doesn't know....

I want to fuck my best
friend's fuck boy.

How Do I Gain Confidence
and not feel like a creep?

Your "Number" Insecuritie

s 3 a Crowd? - Insecurity
and Sexuality

HORNY FEMALE FEMINIST
VIRGIN- I NEED HELP!

I Was Raped By a Teacher and
Slut Shamed Because of It

ng my religious boss and his
ips and tricks??

How to stop thinking about my
boyfriend's ex?

BLACK CATHOLIC BISEXUAL
VIRGIN??

I will always b
of my abortio

ested by my own father

A confident girl?! Run away!

My parents think
because I'm in a

ng asexual gets you
of class???

AM I PENIS SHAMING???

CHRISTIAN ROOMMATE
WON'T LET ME FUCK IN MY
OWN HOME?!?!

SHAME

Oh, you have herpes? You're a
disgusting whore, who deserves
to die alone.

Fat boy confidence in hotty body

I lost my virginity to a groomsr
in a hotel vending machine ha

Asking Dad for Permission to
Marry?!?

Clingy, Jealous, and
insecure?!? HELP.

My Dad is having an affair with
the transgender girl in my class!!!

BLACK
VIRGIN

My mom made me insecure
about threesomes

MY PARENTS ARE SWINGERS
AND I GOT THEIR GENE!!!

We met on Tinder, he threatened to
kill myself and leak my nudes

MMATE
UCK IN MY

Men That Don't Like
Confident Women

PLEASE HELP ME! I am Gender
Fluid and I don't know what to
do about my parent's recent
statements.

I exposed my escort
boyfriend to his parents.

Ruined Christmas with my "slut
behavior"

My dad hires hookers!?

Not All Religions Preach Hate
And Assholery!

My gf wants to fuck when her
parents are in the house

Help! My mom won't stop slut
shaming me!

e ashamed

Molested by my own father

Dear Diary: FUCK

Your "Number" Insecurit

cking My Ex-Boyfriend's Dad

I haven't had sex in 8 years -
where do I start?

I GOT WET SITTING NEXT TO A GUY?!

Rape, Schizophrenia & a
dash of Herpes

Male sexual abuse survivors

If I don't remember if I slept with two guys
last night...Is it bad to not care, or should
I feel slutty? Ps. I don't want to care.

I Stabbed A Guy With a Fork And
Other Weird Stuff I Need Advice
About

I fucked a sex offender??

My long lost sibling
fucked me!

I only fucked you as a joke /
cool slut

MY BOYFRIEND IS GONNA FUCK

Why We're Fucked

A BRIEF INTRODUCTION TO SHAME
AND ITS SHITTY, SHITTY ORIGINS

Ah, shame! It's not only for dogs that have taken a shit on the floor anymore. So who is it for? Well, everyone apparently. Shame is the new black. Fuck. We're totally going to get shamed for saying "black." We didn't mean black racially. Just like the color. Or a lack of color? Black is the absence of color. It's what happens when no visible light reaches the eye. We're not stupid. We know things. What can we say to you to stop this from going viral? Unless going viral will help sell more books. Then we're fine with being shamed for looking stupid. We are *Americans,* after all. Americans, you know, the people constantly shamed worldwide for being shameless. Jesus, this is complicated.

Shame is that voice we hear when we've done something that society deems deceitful, stupid, slutty, un-American, anti-feminist, racist, homophobic . . . the list goes on and on, especially these days. It's the omniscient voice that asks, "Wow, you dumb slut, who in the fuck do you think you are?" (Or some delightful variation on that.) But how can our personal feelings about something we say or do change so significantly based on societal opinion? Are we all just walking around mindlessly speaking and taking action, secretly and silently waiting to

THE EVOLUTION OF SHAME

be reprimanded? Shame is fueled by our deep concern with what others think of us and, perhaps more frighteningly, what we truly think about ourselves. So if self-shame fails to step in and stop us from saying or doing something we want to say or do, we can always count on society to let us know after the fact that we're a real piece of garbage.

Life coach Koren Motekaitis points out that "shame" and "embarrassment" are often used interchangeably, but she reminds us that something truly embarrassing is fleeting and often funny, while shame is a long-lasting belief that you as a person are bad. Shame, she explains, is a tape in your head constantly repeating "I am bad." Shame is also often associated with guilt, but guilt is more isolated. It's that tape again, but this time the tape is telling you "I did something bad."* While both can be oppressive, guilt is many times warranted, and shame is pretty much always a steaming heap of bullshit. Bullshit we've been honing and perfecting for ages.

---

* Koren Motekaitis, "Shame," *How She Really Does It* (podcast), June 10, 2016, http://howshereallydoesit.com/podcast/shame-what-is-it-minisode/.

Historical Roots

Shame is nothing new—it's been used for centuries. And public humiliation as a form of punishment has always been popular in the United States. During the seventeenth century, women who didn't fit the societal norm were accused of witchcraft. Imperfections such as having an extra nipple or mole, not having children, being difficult to get along with, being someone people were envious of, serving spoiled milk, or being poor or of low status were all signs of being a witch. Oh, and if you were a woman who was sexually liberated? To the stakes with you and that witchcraft. Female sexuality in particular has seemed to cause mass panic over the ages, and just as witches were physically hung, sluts are now socially hung. In the 1990s (*cough* Monica Lewinsky *cough*), this shaming really began to rear its ugly head once again. Being accused of being a "slut" has become the modern-day equivalent of being accused of being a witch in Salem of the 1600s—a sexually explorative woman who is shunned and shamed by much of society because they don't fully understand her and therefore she must be dangerous.

We are supposed to learn from our mistakes, so why do the Salem witch trials seem to happen again and again?

We've all seen a movie or TV show set in "the days of yore" in which the criminal is led to the center of town and subjected to mob justice. But have we really evolved from that or have we upgraded the tools we use to do the same exact thing? It seems ochlocracy is still alive and well (or perhaps very unwell). In the United States, we pride ourselves on being a progressive society, but how are body-shaming memes, GIFs, tweets, and soap box Facebook statuses any different from the stocks and pillories of Colonial times? The torture seems to have just become less physical and more mental, which is arguably more dangerous and certainly has a direct correlation to today's staggering suicide statistics, especially amongst our young people. Sally Curtin, a statistician with the National Center for Health Statistics, part of the Centers for Disease Control and Prevention, notes that suicide had been on the decline since 1986 and then suddenly things did a 180. What's happened since 1986, you ask? The Internet. Smartphones. Modern-day scarlet-lettering in the form of a Comments section. Social media isn't just making us feel worse about our bikini bodies and our ability to plate food as well as a Top Chef; it's literally driving us to take our own lives. The shit that was once said about us politely behind our backs is now being said directly to us. And survey says: *we can't fucking take it.*

This is especially true for girls between the ages of ten and fourteen. Although they make up a small percentage of suicides per year, the rate of their demographic experienced the largest percent increase, tripling over fifteen years, from 0.5 to 1.7 per 100,000 people. And of course this statistic just covers suicides, not injuries or attempts.

While stigma, shame, and judgment have always been a part of human life, we've simply swapped out old forms for newer, subtler forms, and the volume of shame and judgment given and received has escalated grotesquely in the age of social media. Scarlet letters are no longer just handed out by the people we know and love. They're given out by the people we don't know and don't love but whose opinions we somehow care about—a lot.

Religion

SOCIETY'S GUILTY NON-PLEASURE

One of the best parts of living in the United States is our obsession with denying ourselves things that bring us pleasure—especially food and sex. We are a country of deny and binge, deny and binge. We go to the all-you-can-eat buffet on our vacation in Las Vegas and then head back to the office on Monday and announce we're on a five-day juice cleanse. Sex is no different. We become single, go on a casual fucking spree, eventually feel nauseated by so many meaningless interaction rituals, and then get mad at ourselves, vowing to not have sex until we've gone on three dates with someone who really means something to us. While going without sex might seem like the bigger problem to most, binging isn't healthy either. Clinical social worker Gerri Luce explains in *Psychology Today*, "Binging on something, be it food or sex or drugs or the Internet, also denies [a person] pleasure because he or she is so intent on acquiring as much as possible as quickly as possible. Any joy is destroyed."[*]

---

[*] Gerri Luce, "Denying Ourselves the Greatest Pleasures of Life," *Psychology Today* online, August 31, 2013, https://www.psychologytoday.com/blog/both-sides-the-couch /201308/denying-ourselves-the-greatest-pleasures-life.

This cycle starts early. Children are often raised in an environment of punishments and rewards, of taking a trip to the treasure chest if they've been good girls and boys all week, and having their TV privileges taken away if they've been naughty. While we all seem very excited to grow up and be "adults" (you know, those people we imagine eat ice cream for breakfast every day and live without the rules of parents), it's pretty apparent that as soon as we escape the reign of our families, we simply pump the brakes on our pleasure. We exit the confines of the family we were born into only to rebuild the confines right up again after we graduate college or move out of our parents' house. We stifle ourselves with jobs that are smart and secure rather than what we love, partners who make us feel not alone rather than alive, and sex lives that feel more comfortable than creative. With so many wild possibilities available to us, we keep choosing the same mediocre options time and time again.

Why do we associate the things that make us feel the best with sin? Why won't we allow ourselves to bask in worldly pleasures? Women especially seem to have a difficult time with this. Probably because our vaginas have been treated like a long-stemmed rose on an episode of *The Bachelorette*—we have only a certain number we can give out, and after that it's over. It's the age-old question "How many pussy licks does it take to get to the slut hidden in all of us?" Oh, wait. That's not a saying. That's just some bullshit society made up one day because, you know, women were getting out of hand.

While religion may be the opiate of the masses, shame is the opiate of sex. Honestly, how kinky can you get when you believe that with every pelvic thrust you become less valuable not only as a mate but also as a person? It's funny—even though women are hyper-sexualized from a young age, people really seem to hate it when we have sex. And that hate is sometimes coming the strongest from the woman in the mirror.

An anonymous Thought Catalog contributor who consistently denies himself pleasure wrote, "Being able to choose what we eat and drink and to give and receive pleasure from another person are holy acts that exercise a person's freedom, and in the case of sex, the mitzvah—or commandment—of creation. This traces back to the enslavement of the Jews in Egypt, where they were not free to experience pleasure at their own wills. God went out of his way to part the sea and deliver the Jews to freedom, so the Jews are commanded to eat, drink, and have sex because not doing so would make God's work for naught."* In other words, enjoying your life is important because the act of enjoyment is the acknowledgment that you lead a life in which you have the privilege to do so.

So did Jesus die for no reason? Was Jesus even a real guy? Did that offend you? Does any of this matter? The "logical"—and we're using that term loosely here—reasons for denying oneself sex or pleasure of any kind seem to be because we don't think we deserve it . . . and possibly because we don't think we can handle it. If we go without long enough, maybe we'll become superhumans who don't need the things the average person needs.

But if we indulge, will 24/7 pleasure be just as torturous as no pleasure at all? To answer this question, let us remind you that if we stop fucking, we humans die out.

Sex Is a Physiological Need

Arousal is a natural, biological response. We don't will ourselves to get horny, we don't turn our nipples on and flip a switch that makes us wet and/or hard. This just happens. Animals fuck without feeling bad. Why don't we?

Animals simply treat sex like business—a business in which the goal is to have the most and best offspring. While humans also want to

---

* Anonymous, "You Should Never Deny Yourself the Pleasure You Deserve," Thought Catalog, April 14, 2014, http://thoughtcatalog.com/anonymous/2014/04/you-should-never-deny-yourself-the-pleasure-you-deserve/.

pass along their genes, we're not really a species known for doing work without proper incentive so, as some theories suggest, evolution gave us the orgasm to ensure we would keep fucking.

When performed consensually and effectively, sex makes us feel good. But is it true—as we may have felt deep in our souls or at least with wishful thinking—that sex is actually *good* for us?

According to "The Relative Health Benefits of Different Sexual Activities," a review by Stuart Brody, Ph.D., of the results from 174 sexual health articles and studies, vaginal-penile intercourse offers a laundry list of benefits. (Unfair as it may seem to same-sex screwing, heterosexual sex keeps us from becoming extinct—it's not that the universe is homophobic, it just needs some of us to be straight, so it offers some bonuses.) P-in-v sex improves vaginal- and pelvic-muscle function, strengthens cardiovascular health, decreases hot flashes in menopausal women, decreases the likelihood of developing breast cancer, lowers susceptibility to stress, and allows a faster recovery from stress.* Some sources even say that semen is a mood booster. Granted, one of those sources is Spike TV, whose male audience might have a slightly biased take on it, but even Sigmund Freud (who, admittedly, turned out to have some problematic theories) believed that using a condom during heterosexual vaginal intercourse negatively affects the orgasm, which then increases the presence of neuroses by disturbing the natural flow of the libido (remember, Freud was fucking obsessed with repression).

While many things can make your pussy tingle or your dick stand at attention, it seems vaginal intercourse has that certain je ne sais quoi. Brody cites a study of young American women in which it was found that the longer a female went without vaginal intercourse, the

---

* Stuart Brody, "The Relative Health Benefits of Activities," *Journal of Sexual Medicine* 7, no. 4, pt. 1 (2010): 1336–61, http://onlinelibrary.wiley.com/doi/10.1111/j.1743 -6109.2009.01677.x/full.

worse she scored on the Beck Depression Inventory (one of the most widely used tests for measuring depression). Furthermore, mood-enhancing effects of vaginal intercourse were nonexistent when condoms blocked the entry of semen into the vagina. And—fuck me harder—even women who rarely or never used condoms but peed right after sex had more depressive symptoms than those who, um, let it linger?

Now, it seems almost irresponsible to share the extensive sperm benefits found in this comprehensive study because, well, unwanted pregnancies, sexually transmitted infections (STIs), and girl power, but, alas, science is like a Twitter follower with no avatar photo—you don't fuck with it. If you're in a committed relationship with a partner who's been tested and you're using some sort of oral or internal contraceptive, you might be able to meditate several minutes less if you go at it raw.

That said, there is also psychological research to back up *all* sex and intimacy as quality of life enhancers (here's looking at you, same-sexers and cuddlers). In fact, sociologist Randall Collins has argued that sex can be explained *only* in a social context. Basically, Collins believes that each person's existence is made up of a series of things he refers to as "interaction rituals" that make our physical existence possible and also give it meaning, and that everything in our lives, including sex, is an interaction ritual. Because of this, by Collins's school of thinking, it is not within the genitals that sexual pleasure is being created but rather through the cooperation and interaction between two people. A study conducted in the early 2000s by researchers Cindy Meston and David Buss revealed that many of the four hundred students they interviewed about having sex were not having it because it physically stimulated them but because of some psychological reason (power, punishment, and pity were all listed as reasons to fuck someone—*fun times!*). As Noam Shpancer, Ph.D., points out, "the deep experience of sexual pleasure depends somehow on the presence, and conduct, of others." And that, little horny ones, is why prostitutes have not been replaced by Fleshlights and blow-up dolls.*

To recap: we are animals whose core purpose is to connect with one another and, yes, mate. It's in our nature! So why, specifically, do we wrap our sexuality and sexual choices in so much shame? Perhaps we are uncomfortable with urges that connect us to other creatures we see as primitive or dirty ("doggy style" isn't necessarily looked at as reverence for man's best friend). And if we're squeamish about simple, straightforward sex, we're even more uncomfortable with the complexities of our deeper sexual selves. Even straight people who enjoy vanilla sex—the "norm"—struggle to come to terms with their sexuality. So what hope do homos have who like their nipples clamped and their butthole tickled?

These are tough questions. And try as we might to answer them, the truth is that sexuality and shame are like fingerprints—everyone's are different and there's no one-size-fits-all solution. As just two individual women, all we can speak to is our own sexual truth and share our own unique perspectives on shame. So from here on out we'll be taking turns on the metaphorical microphone, dishing out our stories, successes, and what-not-to-dos for everything from blow jobs to breakups, in matters of the heart and horniness. Don't worry, you'll know who's speaking with these handy cartoons labeled with our names found at the top of each page.

CORINNE

Krystyna

* Noam Shpancer, "Why Do We Have Sex?," *Psychology Today* online, April 16, 2012, https://www.psychologytoday.com/blog/insight-therapy/201204/why-do-we-have-sex.

Krystyna

Sources of Shame

The Parent Trap

Mom and Dad (and Grandma and Grandpa and Aunt Carol and Aunt Carol's "roommate") really fucked us up. We already blame them for why we can't communicate with our partner, let anyone get close to us, or maintain a steady job, so why not also hold them responsible for all that shame we carry around with us on the reg? While a healthy parenting style can reinforce the natural state of just being okay with who we are and who we want to fuck, parents often project their own insecurities, worries, and fears onto their children. Because, after all, what is a child if not a chance for them to give another human being a much better life than they had and to cancel out all their own failures and shortcomings? Surely that child won't make the same mistakes.

As children, we naturally want to please our parents. The problem with this is, when we get older, even though we're no longer children in the eyes of society, we remain children to our parents, and so we might carry these feelings of inadequacy with us for as long as our parents keep reminding us of them.

I lost my virginity the day I got my braces off. Yep. *That's* how fuckable my teeth are. To me, the braces coming off represented an entrance into womanhood, where I no longer had a lisp and looked like someone's kid sister every time I smiled. So why not attempt to have sexual intercourse with your boyfriend, in his basement, right before his dad comes home from work in the middle of the day? I was sixteen, he was nineteen, and we had been together for three whole magical months at that point. This was nothing like my first technical "relationship" in the eighth grade, with a guy I met at Friendly's and declared was my boyfriend an hour later only to break up with him the following week because I didn't like the way he styled his hair. This was way different. It wasn't the first time a boy had made my heart feel like it was pounding out of my chest, but it was the first time the feeling was mutual. He was a musician, and every time he picked up a guitar and sang a Ryan Cabrera cover, I melted. He made me feel a certain type of electricity that only flows through you the very first time you fall in love and you reach a level of happiness you never knew existed. I expected my parents to give me a hard time about the age difference, even though their age gap was *way* worse. My dad was twenty-eight when he met the tall, blond, blue-eyed stunner that is my mother, shortly after she turned eighteen. I was pleasantly surprised with how well my parents handled me dating an older guy, since they tend to be on the overprotective side, especially my mom. That all came to a screeching halt when I was caught off guard and admitted to my mother that I was no longer a virgin. Woof. She did *not* handle that well. In fact, she handled that in a way that can only be described as severely damaging.

You know when you meet a guy and you're all "OMG! He's the best, most perfect guy in the entire world. I can't even believe some-one this amazing exists and that we found each other and that we're so happy!" And your friends are all "Krystyna, he kinda sucks and he's manipulative and you should seriously break up with him." And you're like *"Shut up, Tiffany. You're just jealous of my perfect relation-ship!"* And then you find out he's been cheating on you for almost the entirety of your seemingly flawless romance? Don't you *hate* when that happens?

My parents suspected this guy was no good. My dad's way of handling those suspicions was to call him by the wrong name on purpose to make it very clear that he had no respect for "Richard? Glen? I can't remember. Sorry."

My mom's way of handling those suspicions was to bottle them up and convince herself that there was no way in hell her teenage daughter was having sex with her boyfriend. This was easy for her, because although she knew I was her teenage daughter, when she looked at me she saw three-year-old Krystyna in a pink tutu singing songs about going to the zoo. I never received a sex talk from my parents, but to be fair, when my mom made a halfhearted attempt to talk about it after walking past a young couple fucking under a sleeping bag on the beach during our family vacation, I immediately got uncomfortable and said, "Yeah, yeah, yeah, I know, I know. I know what that is. They told me at school. It's cool, Mom. I got it covered."

Lies!

I had no idea. In fact, I didn't realize that sex involved the insertion of body parts until the eighth grade. Then in the tenth grade, after watching *Vanilla Sky* at a coed sleepover, I learned that sex was more than one thrust.

I'd like to preface the following story of my mom's reaction to me losing my virginity by saying that despite her bad reaction, she is a gem of a woman and a mother. Hands down the most caring, loving, goofy, adorable human being I have ever met, and I love her dearly. Sometimes parents overreact to things out of fear for their child's safety or emotional well-being—a key fact I was unaware of at the time. That, however, does not make it right.

I believe it was the winter of 2003. My mom wanted to take me, my brother's girlfriend, and my grandmother out to dinner. My grandmother was living with us because she had recently suffered a stroke and now had the mental capacity of a seven-year-old. Grandma fucking thrived in restaurants. I loved going out to eat with her because she would crack me up with her post-stroke shenanigans. Some Grandma Hutchinson gems include walking by everyone's table and asking how their meal is, eating off strangers' plates, taking her dentures out and licking them mid-meal, and—my personal favorite—crying after she finished her dessert and screaming, "But I didn't get nothing to eat! Where's my pie?"

Before Grandma could publicly claim we were starving her at that specific meal, my mom told me a story about a friend of a friend who had a daughter who lived in a big city and would "mess around" with guys. My mom didn't let me use the word "fart" as a child; she made me say "toot" instead. So in her brain, I'm pretty sure "messing around" was code for "fucking raw-dog style." She paused after the story, looked up at me, and asked, "You've never done anything like that, have you, Krystyna?"

I froze. Was not expecting that. I very nervously replied, "Um, well, I mean, ya know. I've had—I've. Yeah. I have."

The look on her face could have scared a fucking ghost. She started to shake and cry, and I'm thinking, *Oh no. What's happening? Are you fucking kidding me?* Then she swiftly stood up, pulled out her chair, and stormed out of the restaurant. *Okay, cool. So she's definitely not kidding.*

There I sat, with my brother's girlfriend and my post-stroke grandmother, who was in the middle of licking her dentures like a lollipop and asking where the chocolate pie was. I just sat there in silence, trying to comprehend what I was feeling. I had disappointed my mother so much that she couldn't even sit across the table from me. I felt like a broken person.

When we got home, my mother ran into her room, locked her door, and didn't speak to me for a few days. I wish I could say that I knew then her reaction was inappropriate and far too intense for the situation, but I was genuinely crushed and confused. Is sex this horrible thing that makes parents emotionally abandon their children for a brief period of time? Is my dad going to react like this? Am I now that girl in

The Scarlet Letter? What the fuck? When I had decided to have sex for the first time, it was a decision I made with certainty and excitement. A decision I felt really good about. After dinner that night, all those emotions unraveled and turned into shame, confusion, and anxiety.

Her reaction taught me two things: (1) I needed to start protecting my mom from emotional agony by lying to her, and (2) sex was something you needed to hide from people, especially your parents, because they'll be disappointed in you when they eventually find out. That night was the start of a very long journey into discovering who the fuck I was as a daughter, woman, and sexual being. Part of me was angry and wanted to rebel against my mom for not minding her own business and judging me the same way the bitchy girls who bullied me in middle school did. What right did she have to try to demean my sexuality?

My mom and I grew distant for a while after that because I could never tell if what I was doing at the moment would eventually cause her to explode and emotionally abandon me. It was as if I were experiencing a minor level of PTSD. Did it stop me from being sexual with my boyfriend? Hell no. But it did stop me from asking my mom questions when I really needed her advice. It stopped me from telling a lot of my friends about my sex life. And it stopped me from being confident in the decisions I made with my body. I unconsciously had learned to take action and make decisions based on the approval and happiness of others.

The heartache that consumed me after finding out my then-boyfriend was cheating on me as I was falling madly in love with him was paralyzing, but it was nothing compared to how I felt that night at the restaurant. As I grew older and looked back at that moment in my life from a rational adult's perspective, I realized I still had no clue as to why the hell she reacted that way. But the part of me that wanted answers was shut down by the possibility of revisiting something that had traumatized me so much.

When Corinne and I started *Guys We Fucked,* one of my first thoughts was *No way in hell I'm telling my mom about this!* I remember talking to my brother about the podcast, and the first words out of his mouth were, "Ha! Hope Mom never finds out about this!" I shrugged it off. "Oh, please. She doesn't even know what a podcast is. Plus, not a lot of people listen to it, so I don't know how she could even find out about it." Shortly after that talk, much to my horror and surprise, the podcast got popular. We started getting all this incredible press, with zero help from a PR person. I remember Emma Gray of *The Huffington Post* interviewed us, and the title of the article was "Meet the Women Changing How We Think About Female Sexuality, One Sex Story at a Time." I almost cried when I read that. We were asked to do a motherfucking TED Talk! We were interviewed on television, and I had tears of joy rolling down my face as my friends and I gathered at a bar downtown to watch the segment the night it aired. Everything I had dreamt of as a little girl—and beyond—was actually coming true. I was so fucking happy and proud of myself and Corinne. But because of the title of the podcast, I couldn't share *any* of this with my mom. All I had ever wanted was to make my parents proud, and when I finally experienced the type of success that most people only dream about, I had to jump through hoops to hide it from them. Then one day, almost three years into doing the podcast, my brother called me and said, "Mom knows. I tried to tell her how successful it is, but she's pretty upset." My heart sank to the floor as I mentally prepared for her to not talk to me for a while. Eventually we did talk, but this time around I had the emotional tools to deal with it and calmly communicate my feelings to her. It didn't just bring us closer together; I finally got the answers to the questions I had been too afraid to ask after that night at the restaurant. In a matter of minutes, the pieces of a puzzle I had spent over ten years trying to solve all fell into place.

Krystyna's Mom's Side of the Story

Despite growing up with a wonderful and loving family, I was sexually assaulted multiple times by multiple people from the age of eight to fourteen. The boyfriend I was with for three years in high school physically assaulted me during the entirety of our relationship.

Up until recently, I only shared those experiences with my husband. Thanks to Krystyna, this past year I have come to realize that the bullying, sexual abuse, and physical abuse I suffered as a young girl made me extremely protective of her, even smothering. I acted the way I did because I was determined to make sure that she would never have to endure what I went through. What I didn't realize was that trying to keep her sheltered from traumatic experiences would also cut off our ability to have important conversations about healthy sex.

Because of my overly conservative attitude toward sexuality, Krystyna did not share her podcast with me for over two years. She knew I would be very upset and felt it was best not to share this with me—which I totally understand. Especially given my less than favorable reaction after finding out she was no longer a virgin at the age of sixteen. Over the past few years, when Krystyna would come home to visit, I could feel her desire to share her world with me—but I also felt her hesitation. I was almost afraid to know what she was doing, so I didn't ask. I felt a wedge between us, but I didn't know what to do about it.

Then one day I was on Facebook and saw a photo of Corinne and Krystyna on my feed. Underneath the photo read "Guys We Fucked," and I just about passed out. Up till then, I had no idea of the podcast's name. Krystyna only had informed me that it had to do with sexuality. I was shocked, to say the least. I could not understand how it was true. I didn't bring her up to talk like that, and I'd never heard her speak in a lewd tone. What happened to my little girl who used to dance around our living room in a tutu singing "On the Good Ship Lollipop"? I was brokenhearted. I was also very concerned about what my close friends would think. They all had loved Krystyna since she was a baby. How would they react? I never talked to anyone about it. I didn't even tell Krystyna that I knew.

Usually the parent teaches their children about life. Well, in this case, my daughter taught me. She taught me to not judge a book by its cover (pun intended). We eventually discussed the title, and she invited me to be a guest on the podcast. Krystyna opened the door to her world, and I finally decided to walk through. *Wow* is all I can say. I felt guilty that it took me so long to enter that door, but I am so glad I did. I finally opened my mind and saw how happy she was doing what she loved most in this world and making a career out of it. As a parent, you want your children to follow their heart, see their dreams come true, and just be *happy*.

When I opened myself up and ventured into her world without judgment, I quickly understood that she *is* following her heart and making her dreams come true in a way that expresses who she really is. As always, what she does is done with love and compassion for the human race. After I was on the podcast and read e-mails from their listeners around the world who related to my story, I realized that my daughter had not changed at all; she'd grown into a woman. A beautiful woman with a beautiful heart. ∎

As we get older, we all start putting together the puzzle pieces and answering all the open-ended questions we've been accumulating since childhood. Questions about how life works and why we sometimes love people who don't respect us and what happens when we die and how come Santa Claus mimics my dad's handwriting when he comes to *my* house and he mimics Katy's dad's handwriting when he's at *her* house? Hearing about my mom's past was one of the biggest aha! moments of my life. It taught me to dig deeper whenever I feel like there's a missing piece to the puzzle, instead of what I normally did, which was to assume it was my fault that I didn't fully grasp the situation and beat myself up over it. That's not productive for anyone.

Corinne and I recently received an e-mail from a seventeen-year-old female listener living in the South. She was beside herself because her mom and stepdad had a rule that not only was she not allowed to leave the house wearing shorts, but she wasn't allowed to leave her *bedroom* wearing shorts. Her mother had told her that dressing that way in public meant she was "asking for attention" and that she would "eventually get raped because guys can't control themselves." Two years ago my reaction to that e-mail would have been along the lines of "What the actual fuck is your mom thinking? That's some manipulative, sexist bullshit," etc. But immediately upon reading her e-mail, my newly formed spidey sense went off and the answer jumped out at me. This girl's mother was acting out of fear. What may truly have been intended as an act of love to keep her daughter safe was coming to the surface as illogical and extremely controlling. Fear of what, I wasn't exactly sure. Maybe she had been raped. Maybe she had caught her husband looking at her daughter, or at another teenage girl, in a strange or creepy way, and instead of talking to him about it, she was protecting her kid from potentially being molested. The only possible clue the girl had given me was that her parents were thirty-one years old. She equated that to "It's not like they're generations older than me and out of touch!" and I equated that to "Your mom had you when she was fourteen, and she's scared you'll be a young mother like her and fuck up your life." No matter what the actual answer was, the mother's intentions were misguided, even if they stemmed from a loving place.

Finding out that your parents aren't perfect is a tough realization to process, but I encourage you to lovingly find the missing puzzle pieces if you can. It may take ten years, but the aha! moment of finally understanding their intentions might help ease a traumatic memory or two.

CORINNE

Wine Me, Dine Me, Say Something About My Weight

While parents sometimes just don't understand, you can't blame them for every shortcoming. At a certain point it's time to take the steering wheel of your own life and, ya know, find someone else to blame! May I suggest *the person you're fucking*? This source of shame is a hard one to admit, because who wants to reveal that the person with whom you feel you can be your true self is a person who is unconsciously making you feel like your true self isn't good enough? While you may have no problem with a partner who subtly nudges you to be the best version of yourself, you may have a big problem with someone who slowly coaxes you to morph into a person you are not and never planned to be. But it's not just committed relationships that can manifest shame; it's every sexual interaction.

Fucked If You Do, Fucked If You Don't

I don't feel shame a ton. I never have. Not sure why, just #blessed, I guess. But the one time I decided to have a one-night stand (I know—

unbelievably, I've only had one), the person definitely tried his darned-est to shame the fuck outta me.

It had been a rough night. Even for a stand-up comedian living on $19,000 a year in New York City. I had been asked by a friend to perform at his birthday roast at a faux comedy venue in TriBeCa. For those unfamiliar with the intricacies of comedy, if someone tells you they're performing at a comedy club with the word "lounge" in its title, they're not performing at a comedy club at all. More likely than not, they'll be holding a microphone in the midst of bridge-and-tunnelers drunk on Long Island iced teas. (I love Long Island iced teas and order them all the time. I'm also from New Jersey.) If it's a really good gig, they'll be standing on a raised wooden platform. If it's less good, perhaps a milk crate.

While the roasts they do on Comedy Central are accurate repre-sentations of just how brutal roasts can be, what one must not forget is that fame and money really ease the blow of being publicly called a whore and, worse yet, a hack. So I've heard. As a comedian, I should've recalled the old Friars Club rule of only roasting the ones we love, but instead I let my mind be clouded by my egocentric need for stage time and a Facebook status boasting that I was doing something cool in the world of comedy on a Saturday night. And so I went. Like a pig stupidly accepting an invitation to a luau "just to enjoy the party," I fucking went.

I would say I have a significantly higher level of self-confidence than the average comic, but contrary to my public persona, I'm not made of stone. After being told in front of a crowd of strangers that my comedy is like "spoken word poetry," then bombing my own set, proving the previous roaster right, it was explained to the audience that I was "proof that women aren't funny" and, furthermore, "the width of my vagina was constantly expanding due to the amount of comedic cock that had been inside."

Left with an aftertaste in my mouth worse than SlimFast's (high school was weird), I made an honest twenty-first-century mistake and texted a comic I knew only from Twitter, asking him to meet me for a drink.

I often reprimand Krystyna for her naïveté in thinking that anyone with a dick (who likes to stick that dick in vaginas) enjoys her platonic company, but choking on the post-bomb smoke, I became distracted and conveniently forgot my own golden rule.

Although I knew him only in doses of 140 characters or less, Ronnie (not his real name) had a certain socially unacceptable charm that drew me to him. He was rude, he was creepy, he obviously had more issues with women than Eminem, but he was funny and he was forward, and I couldn't think of anyone else I would possibly want to get hammered with on a shitty Saturday night.

Ronnie was unlike anyone I have ever experienced. He was cute, but from the start he rode that fine line between regular-guy charming and Ted Bundy charming, which I must admit intrigued me more than it terrified me. He led me down the streets of SoHo with the implication that he had his mind set on a great spot, but it became clearer and clearer that he had not a fucking clue. Finally, in a mix of my feet throbbing from the unexpected amount of walking I had just done in heels and my intense need for a Maker's on the rocks after Ronnie had asked me for the seventh time if we could have sex, we ended up at the front bar of the SoHo Room.

Much to the shock of the old-school bartender who took our order, but not at all to the shock of me, Ronnie ordered his drink first and then made me pay for mine. I really had no problem with this. After all, it was I who had asked him to meet up, with no intentions of getting naked. Going Dutch was the appropriate payment plan for the night I had in mind. Apparently, Ronnie thought his poor-man's Ben Affleck in rags look was going to make me wet enough to add him to my iPhone "Guys I Fucked" list. Little did he know I've always been a Matt Damon girl. Upon realizing that me having the ass of a Puerto Rican girl did not his J.Lo make me, Ronnie left me in the bar, with half a glass of whiskey, to fuck an open mic-er he had waiting around the corner as backup. There I was, stranded in a bar mid-drink, because I wouldn't fuck a comedy colleague I had just met that night.

I'm crazy, but not crazy enough to waste nine dollars' worth of Maker's Mark. After all, times were tough. Luckily for me, a girl left alone at a bar in New York City is never alone for long. Soon I was chatting with the sexy, pierced cocktail waitress and three dudes from New Jersey who definitely had done their fair share of gymming, tanning, and laundry-ing. On any other night, presented with this socialization option or slowly inserting bamboo shoots underneath my fingernails, I would opt for bamboo shoots every time, but there was something about how the moon was shining and how the music was playing, and, oh yeah, how fast I was drinking that whiskey that made this situation not only tolerable but enjoyable.

I am not a people person. Anyone who knows me can attest to the fact that I've hidden in hampers to avoid conversations. Okay, a singular hamper, but still, it happened. For some reason, however, that night I had morphed not only into a people person but into a *delightful* people person who had caught the eye of the sexiest of the three Garden State dudes. His name was Anthony and he was from Atlantic City. Naturally, he was also the least interesting of the bunch, but Mama had had her fill of independent film protagonist behavior for the night and just needed some dense testosterone. So Mama gave the okay when Anthony asked her if she wanted to go barhopping with them. (I'm Mama, BTW.)

Whatever you're picturing in your mind right now, that's exactly what Anthony from Atlantic City looked like. If you're still unclear, to put it into perspective, if you've never worn sweatpants to a bar, you're not Anthony from Atlantic City. He bought me bottled Bud Light after bottled Bud Light and grinded up against me in that way that really makes you ask yourself, "Is this guy gay?" We started making out, and he was a god-awful kisser, which should always set off an alarm in one's mind, but I am known 'round these parts for ignoring alarms. In fact, if as a guy approaches me I don't hear so many alarms that I think a reggaeton song is playing, I'm not interested. I continually repeated to myself, *Corinne, do not go home with this guy. Corinne, do not go home with this guy. Corinne, do not go home with this guy.*

As the cab pulled up to Anthony's apartment, I gasped audibly. *So this is why people go into boring things like banking,* I thought. Although it was in TriBeCa (no thank you), his apartment building was so beautiful I would've paid admission just to go inside. We took the elevator up to a spacious yet void-of-character three-bedroom apartment that Anthony shared with two other equally dull and vain people.

I should probably remind you right about now that we are currently in the middle of the story of my first and only one-night stand. What I should've known about one-night stands, but didn't, is that they are very clinical. There's no ice cream eating, there's no Netflix watching. The guy really just wants you to get right to it. The pussy, however, is not a car that can be turned on by remote control from the parking lot. It is an antique vehicle whose engine must be revved. Anthony failed to catch on, so at one point I just excused myself to the bathroom, splashed some water into my vagina, and instructed my little pink friend to get this party started.

While I was riding the high of fucking someone other than a comic (i.e., someone good-looking), I was mere moments away from being reminded why I love fucking comics. Comics are freaks in bed because we're out of our fucking minds. For example, I like to choke people. I'm not talking, like, Boston Strangler here; every experienced choker knows that you want to start at the looseness of a pendant-style necklace and then slowly move to the tightness of a puka shell necklace. If the person starts losing consciousness, you've gone too far. God bless his soul, Anthony went along with my choking, but I could tell he wasn't that into it. So he attempted to spice things up with dirty talk.

Anthony's version of dirty talk was asking me, "When's the last time you had sex?"

"Yesterday," I replied. Because it was after midnight. In reality, I had had sex that morning, but I'm a stickler for technicalities.

Anthony did not like that answer. "Ew, that's disgusting. What, do you do this all the time?" And just like that, I got kicked out of Anthony's apartment mid-sex. Because I have too much sex.

I don't know if you've ever had to remove yourself from someone's erect penis to then pay for a cab from TriBeCa to Harlem, but it really knocks you down a peg. It's a dismount you will not ever forget. It's like Kerri Strug in the 1996 Olympics. You land it, but you know in your heart that it's your last hurrah as you stumble all the way home.

The world seems to be filled with these two very conflicting messages: "Be who you are" vs. "Don't be a dumb, fat whore." But . . . what if you are a dumb, fat whore? What if that's your truth? It appears that the real message we're being told is "Accept yourself, but only if you're acceptable."

CORINNE

Slut-Shaming

As women, we often feel sexually suffocated by society because a sexual woman is a free woman and that's no good for order. But also it seems females cannot all feel free and sexual harmoniously. Even when we're able to get the men feeling comfortable with our sexuality, many of us still shun the sexual choices of our sisters because we think *their* freedoms might showcase *our* shortcomings.

As somewhat of an expert, or at least as someone with a lot of practice in getting dicks hard, I can assure you there are very few things you can do to make a guy not want to fuck you. I've worn ugly shoes, revealed my flat chest, not worn makeup, talked about my feelings, and even gotten my period like the savage I am, yet still I continue to slay peen.

What I will say is that while I am very grateful for my podcast "fame," while I continued to be a top-choice booty call during the first two years of the podcast, men rarely wanted to be my *boyfriend*. I realized I was subtly being slut-shamed because I was the host of an anti slut-shaming podcast. How very meta. As I learned the hard way, the stigma of the sexually seasoned woman is still alive and well . . . and while the easy target is the men who are not bringing me home to meet their mothers, I blame my *own* sex for this outdated institution not being extinct.

Sister Blister

In times of duress, oppressed groups have historically stuck together. I think I'd be hard-pressed to find a black person who pooh-poohs the importance of Black Lives Matter, yet every night I perform for comedy club audiences whose female population refuses to so much as raise their hand when I ask "Are there any feminists in the room?" The silence I am greeted with is undoubtedly a direct result of fear. Fear that by a woman admitting she is just as powerful as the man sitting next to her, the dick of aforementioned man might be a little less hard in the bedroom later that night. In our quest to find mates, we are continually and repeatedly losing ourselves.

Women should truly be congratulated. We have tyrannized ourselves like no other group in history through our silence, our cattiness, and our insecurities. On any given day you can witness countless woman-on-woman hate crimes, from rude commentary on a fellow sister's short shorts to an evil eye for even looking at a stranger's boyfriend. You might not realize it, but we have been in the midst of our own emotional genocide for years.

If you're a woman reading this, think of the last time you did something shitty to another woman. What was the impetus? Did it have something to do with a man? I'll bet my burned bra it did. Individually, we're adults with great jobs, amazing minds, strong bodies, and endless potential, but in unison we're still those catty girls who are saving men time and energy by keeping *ourselves* down. To quote Tina Fey's character in *Mean Girls,* "You all have got to stop calling each other sluts and whores. It just makes it okay for *guys* to call you sluts and whores."

Shame is something women are taught to feel early on. And while it's currently taboo to make *anyone* feel ashamed about anything, shame does have its place. We shouldn't feel ashamed if we were raped or had an abortion or even ate an entire box of Oreos in one sitting, but we *should* feel ashamed of how many times we've thrown a fellow female under the bus for the amount of cleavage she exposed at the office holiday party, for blowing that guy without having gone to dinner with him first, or for openly admitting she doesn't agree with the possibly antiquated practice of monogamy.

So is it annoying when guys spread their sausage thighs too widely on public transportation and is it gross that we have to consider if it's worth the hassle to wear *yoga pants* to *yoga class*? Yes. Men, fucking control yourselves. But what's *inexcusable* is women terrorizing one another in a world that's already a war zone for our kind. It's always been pretty clear to me that we are the stronger sex, but our Achilles' heel was, is, and continues to be men. To quote my favorite Alanis Morissette song (yes, I went there), "Sister blister we fight to please the brothers, we think their acceptance is how we win / They're happy we're climbing over each other, to beg the club of boys to let us in."

Our ingrained hatred of one another doesn't just affect us in the halls of our high schools and offices; it hurts us even politically. During the 2016 election, we treated Hillary Rodham Clinton like our least favorite Real Housewife. Many women I know called her a bitch and a cunt. And on Election Day, they voted for her but then left the voting station and trashed her on social media. Whether we're judging the homecoming queen or selecting our president, we morph into the monsters men think we are to one another. We nitpick the women around us because it's a relief from being nitpicked by society. We nitpick because we somehow have the idea that by doing so we are making ourselves look better, when really we're just making ourselves look worse. Every stab of the knife into another woman becomes a step up for a man on the ladder of the patriarchy.

I've said it before, I'm gonna say it now, and I'm gonna continue saying it: We women must be better to one another. Over-the-top nice to one another. Kind when it seems unnecessary and borderline lesbionic.

I'm not saying that we should be nicer to someone just because she's a woman, but . . . well, yes, I am.

Thus, I present to you:

THE TEN SISTERHOOD COMMANDMENTS (ER, STRONG SUGGESTIONS)

1. Thou shalt not use the weaknesses of other women as a step stool to elevate ourselves. There is room enough for us all to succeed.

2. Thou shalt not make a fellow woman feel bad for being her best self. The world would be a lot better if we all were our best selves.

3. Thou shalt remember the negative things we say about women are more of a reflection of how we feel about ourselves. Calling someone else ugly only shows how ugly we really are.

4. Thou shalt not fuck a person who is in a monogamous relationship with a fellow woman, whether or not the woman is someone you know. Extend others the same courtesy you would hope they would extend to you.

5. Thou shalt stop commenting on other women's bodies, positively or negatively. You're probably not a doctor.

6. Thou shalt compliment little girls for more than being pretty or having a beautiful dress, and thou shalt compliment adult women for more than having great legs or cute shoes. There's nothing wrong with caring about beauty and fashion, but being a woman is so much more than appearance.

7. Thou shalt be honest, in the interest of your fellow woman's protection, not for your personal satisfaction. Harsh truths can be crucial for someone's safety, but a lot of the time you're probably just being a bitch.

8. Thou shalt stop saying "Yas Queen." We stole that from gay men anyway.

9. Thou shalt wear underwear when trying on bathing suits. We know there's that hygiene sticker, but if your pussy touches the sticker and then *my* pussy touches the sticker, what's the fucking point of the sticker?

10. Thou shalt be cognizant of the amount of time we spend talking about boy problems. We have so much to achieve and so much time to make up for.

Once you've stopped attacking the people who should be your biggest allies, grab a sponge because it's time to scrub off all the shame that's been undoubtedly slathered on you over the years—for what you look like, how you speak, what you know, what you do, what you think, and most definitely who, how, why, where, and how much you fuck. *Fuck*.

Strong-Shaming Is the New Slut-Shaming

I don't recall ever meeting an insecure baby. I've met a baby who vomited on me within the first hour of us being together, one who pooped while looking straight into my eyes, and another who knocked a dish full of spaghetti onto the floor, zero fucks given, but never one who insisted she keep her T-shirt on at the pool. Babies do what they want to do when they want to do it without a care in the world. I mean, as soon as I learned to use my legs I ran around the house naked, *espe-*

cially when company was over, and somehow I am confident enough to still be naked in public today. In fact, I performed stand-up fully nude in front of my peers a few years ago.

Everyone likes to shit on "cockiness," and it's no wonder why—everyone is so fucking insecure. People are constantly turned off by my "cockiness," and those people are—you guessed it—insecure. I'm still not nearly close to the level of success I fully intend on achieving, but even when Krystyna and I first started experiencing small triumphs, peers would say things to me like "Wow, you've really changed. You're kind of a bitch now that you're doing well." *Au contraire, mon frère,* I was *always* confident—which is what most people mean when they call a woman a "bitch." Those people just never cared to notice before because I had no value to them. We are in a business of hashtags, headlines, and hot topics, so when I was doing open mics in basements, my big ego wasn't casting a noticeable shadow. The whole room was already dark.

It's almost a cliché at this point, but people really do have a deep dislike of confident women. A quick Google search of the phrase "people hate a confident woman" brought me to a blog called *Alpha Game.* Yes, this is the most press the *Alpha Game* blog will ever get, and that's probably a mistake on my part, but, hey, I also recently decided what size couch I should order by "eyeballing" it. Furthermore, so many books on feminism and women's studies only quote highbrow sources or major social and political figures, but that's not how most people think. As much as we liberals—with our upturned, pierced noses—might consider sources like the one I'm about to quote "bottom feeders," I think this is a far more accurate look into the mind of the average dude lurking on the Internet.

A contributor to *Alpha Game* with the screen name "VD" (insert crying laughing face emoji here) posted an article he bluntly titled "Why Normal Men Hate Strong Women." This is my favorite excerpt (and, please, read what I have to say afterward before you start Instagramming this without all the information):

When people say that men "can't handle" strong women, they're half missing the point. It's not that men can't do it, it's that they don't want to do it. When I hear "strong" or "intelligent" woman, my first thought is "Ah, she's a constant pain in the ass to everyone around her."

Because, rightly or wrongly, they feel inferior, that sort of woman is constantly trying to prove she is "strong enough" or "smart enough." And try-hard women aren't any more attractive or pleasant to be around than try-hard men. My reaction to a try-hard woman trying to prove herself is usually to ask "for what?" Strong enough for what? Smart enough for what?*

I chose this particular section because I don't fully disagree with it. Many men *are* put off by women who bust their balls, speak their minds, and generally act like equals. Some men like a challenge, and those are the men I date. But a high percentage of men don't want to be bothered. Why make life more difficult than it already is? In a way, I get it. Part of the reason I don't want kids is because I imagine the hassle will outweigh the reward. Maybe a "difficult woman" is comparable.

The catch here is, *we all need to be more difficult* (i.e., our own fucking people). If you had the option of getting to a store by walking down a flat sidewalk or by hiking up a mountain, how would you go to the store? Most of us would use the sidewalk, *but* if the only way to get to the store was by hiking up that mountain and you truly wanted to get something from the store, you would lace up your boots, grab a stick, and start hiking. Once the act of being unapologetically ourselves is seen as less of a hike, we'll all be able to relax a little. There are

---

* VD, "Why Normal Men Hate Strong Women," *Alpha Game* (blog), July 21, 2015, http://alphagameplan.blogspot.com/2015/07/why-normal-men-hate-strong -women.html.

still too many women on the planet who value being with a man more than they value being their own person. This isn't only dangerous for the individual woman; it's a danger to all women in a society where women already hold less value than men. Whether you identify as a woman, a man, or nonbinary, the first step in not getting mind-fucked is recognizing your value and demanding that other people who want to be a part of your life recognize it as well.

Fucks Given

A LESSON IN SELF-LOVE

CORINNE

On February 18, 2014, I ceased to be a private person. Which is great for someone who (like Andy Warhol) has always dreamed of being famous but terrible for someone who (like Helen Mirren) doesn't care what you think. That was the day journalist, and my friend, Rich Goldstein published the first of many pieces about *Guys We Fucked: The Anti Slut-Shaming Podcast.* In a photo accompanying the article, entitled "The Podcast Too Hot for iTunes," I was seductively sucking on a colorful lollipop next to Krystyna, who was eye-fucking readers from beneath the brim of her gray beanie. This article changed our careers. It got us a fan following, got us the attention of the very cliquey NYC comedy scene, and even helped us become (after a long censorship battle with iTunes) the first podcast with "fuck" written out in its title, not abbreviated. But our newfound location atop an Internet milk crate also gave me a lot to think about in terms of relationships, sexuality, and, unexpectedly, the unsolicited opinions of total strangers.

I hate the saying "Everyone is beautiful." It's not true, and it discredits people who actually are. I know the saying is supposed to cover all types of beauty—the outside kind and the inside kind—but

I feel like in the past few years PC culture has been trying to make a claim that *everyone* is *aesthetically* beautiful. Not only is that asinine; it also perpetuates the myth that being outwardly beautiful or even feeling outwardly beautiful is an integral point of human existence. *Beauty isn't fucking everything,* yet we have been taught as a culture that, especially for women and gay men, it is *mostly* everything.

I have friends who are prettier than me and friends who are uglier than me. My ugly friends (aren't I a delight?) don't talk a lot about wanting to be more attractive, but my pretty friends talk somewhat regularly about how annoying it is to be valued primarily for their looks. The grass is always greener, right? I often think about wishes, because I'm a dreamer at heart, and time and time again I ask myself, "If a magic genie popped out of a bottle today and gave me the choice to be smarter, prettier, or funnier, which would I choose?" Smarter and funnier rotate, but prettier is always, always last. After thirty-one years on this Earth, I just know it wouldn't help anything. Plus, I like my face no matter how many people on Instagram disagree.

Speaking of which, here's what they think, and notice the theme here:

This upsets me—not because it hurts my feelings but because what does all this even mean? Why would I be "cuter" or "hotter"? I'm confident in myself, my sexuality, and my looks. But am I not allowed to feel confident because I'm not aesthetically "perfect" (whatever that means)? Are only "10s" allowed to be confident?

Good news, I am a 10. In fact, I'm an 11, because my ratings system isn't based solely on my silhouette. Why is this unfathomable to most people? Most distressingly, how can a mentally stable woman think these are acceptable comments to leave on a fellow female's social media? By all means, critique my words or challenge my statements, but after all I have achieved, do I still have to sit here and be judged by my selfies? I thought these were my fans? This is some Selena (the dead one) level shit.

So, what does this have to do with "loving yourself first"? Well, a lot. Much of our self-love, especially that of women, is based on how others perceive us, and others' initial perception is based almost entirely on looks. This is all wrong. Self-love should, as the word implies, come from within; therefore the opinions of others should not be factors in the affair you ultimately want to be having with yourself, and a mirror should merely reflect your face, not your self-worth.

To get yourself out of this tangled web, you must first digest the fact that *what other people think does not matter*. This one sounds simple enough in theory, but it's not. It might take months or even years to digest, but it is well worth the effort. You will be gifting yourself a lifetime of freedom. I don't care if you give yourself a two-minute pep talk while staring at your face in the mirror each morning, meditate, masturbate, write an autobiographical love poem, or bind the "haters" like you're Sarah from *The Craft*. You have to stop caring about what other people think. (Side note: if you've never seen *The Craft*, that's a big part of your self-love problem right there.)

I never really gave much of a flying fuck about the opinions of others. I was knocking bitches out the way in gymnastics class at age five. But I *completely* stopped caring about what other people thought of me based on one incident that spanned one day in the sixth grade.

Always looking for inspiration via my fashion idol Melissa Joan Hart, I had been watching an episode of *Sabrina the Teenage Witch* and spotted one of her brunette buddies donning one black knee sock and . . . wait for it . . . one *white* knee sock. Holy fuck, I had to try this. So the next day when I got ready for school I put on one black knee sock and one white sock and mentally prepared to blow the minds of all those peasants lurking in the halls of Burnet Middle School.

Things, um, didn't go quite as expected. Based on the looks I was getting, you would've honestly thought I had come to school that day covered in my own feces. It got to the point where one of my best friends—let's call her Alyssa—*refused to walk next to me.* That day ended with me hysterically crying after school in Ms. Roger's arms. And I vowed to never again ruin a kind teacher's silk shirt with tears.

I think everyone has a moment like KneeSockGate, a moment when we realize there are repercussions for *just being ourselves.* The problem is, most people choose to make sure an incident like this never occurs again by masking their true selves rather than paying the penance for being who they are. (Cue self-hatred.)

I've always been confused by people who hate themselves, but it made perfect sense once I realized that they, for the most part, are not being themselves. If I had a stranger at the reins of my soul, I would also not like me. Because I wouldn't be me. And that leads me perfectly into my next point: *people are stupid.*

If you find yourself having a lot of trouble with not caring what other people think of you, just remember, people, as a group, are fucking morons. Need help with that idea? Well, just to whet your whistle: for years we had no inkling smoking cigarettes might be bad for us, we've watched as species after species has gone extinct, we've burned our fellow humans alive based on rumors of them being witches, and we decided it would be good if different countries used different methods of measurement so we can all be confused all the fucking time.

This doesn't just apply to generic groups of anonymous humans. You need to include the most important individuals in your life too: friends, parents, bosses—no one gets a free pass to Fucksville. I'm not saying you shouldn't pause for a sec if someone is worried you might be doing something truly unhealthy or dangerous, but really be selective. For example, at any given time in my life I would say I care about what approximately five people think. These people have been carefully vetted through intense secret-keeping challenges, my study of their behavior during mental breakdowns I occasionally release from the vault, and my judging basically every move they make and grading them on character merit. Even after all this, I still hold complete veto power.

The parents part of the "people are stupid" equation understandably always seems to get everyone into a real pickle. We all kinda sorta want to do right by our folks, whether they're the POTUS or currently incarcerated. We all want the achievements in our lives—big and small—to mean enough that our parents will want to hang them on the metaphorical refrigerator. But may I recommend viewing your parents as the imperfect beings they are? Not to the point where you lose respect for them, but enough to humanize them. Sit outside the bathroom and listen to your mom have vicious post-Thanksgiving diarrhea, stare down your dad as he watches an episode of *Dance Moms* and gets too into it, and rejoice in knowing your parents are simply basic bitches. Just like everyone else. To quote my mother, "Even President Bill Clinton has gotten poop on his hand while wiping." We all have. We're fucking disgusting.

Krystyna

Feeling Femasculated

I met Stephen in the summer of 2010 after I was cast as one of the leads in a music video he was directing on Long Island. The first day of the shoot, he drove me to the set. We endured a long car ride—just the two of us—in heavy traffic from New York City and filled almost every second of it with getting-to-know-you conversation. One of the first things I found out about him was that he was in a relationship with a famous porn star named Stoya. I, like every person upon finding out this information, immediately Googled her on my phone. Was she a MILF? Did she have huge fake titties with rock-hard nipples that looked like someone was staring at you with their eyes crossed? Was she porn-star hot or was she regular-person hot? Did she cake on the makeup and flaunt her butt cleavage? Nope, none of that. She had the face of Megan Fox. And the body of Megan Fox. And every other link that came up on Google was some brilliant think piece she wrote on the ins and outs of sexuality. I was impressed and wanted to know *everything*. "How'd you meet her?!" "What's the sex like?" "Can you fuck other people?" "Has she met your parents?" And another question I had in my head but felt was too inappropriate to ask, given I had only known him for ninety minutes at that point: *Are you incredible at sex?!* I wanted to know every little detail, and, boy, did I get it. It was one of the most fascinating road-trip conversations of my life. This guy was the man!

Fast-forward a year and a half. Stephen and I didn't talk after the video shoot because we had no reason to. Then, out of the blue, he e-mailed me, asking to get lunch and talk comedy, in hopes of involving me in an upcoming comedic video he was working on. I was so excited to see him and talk more about the porn-star thing! We met a few days later in the East Village at one of those weekend brunch spots with an hour wait. There was never any small talk between Stephen and I, which is part of what intrigued me about him. But I wouldn't allow myself to have a crush on him because of the whole girlfriend thing. By the time we sat down at a table, I excitedly asked, "So how's your porn-star girlfriend?!" He looked down at his plate, bummed out, and responded, "She just dumped me last week." To which I responded, "Ohhhhhhh, is that so?!?!?" I'd like to think I hid my excitement over our future life together that may or may not include a bunch of babies, but I royally suck at hiding how I feel. My eyes and ears perked up as if I had been on a juice cleanse for a month and someone just put a stack of chocolate chip pancakes in front of me. He described his heartache as I tried so hard to conceal my happiness over his newfound single-dom. That one-hour brunch "meeting" turned into a ten-hour day date. We walked around and talked, we went to a museum and talked, we went to a cupcake shop and talked, we took a cab across town and talked. When I returned to my apartment later that evening, I did something completely out of character for me. I called my mom and said, "Guess what? I met my future husband today!" I mark that day as our anniversary because it's the day I started falling in love with him.

While my feelings for Stephen were blossoming, all those cool little facts I had learned about his now ex that had originally impressed and intrigued me started to plague me with the grossest type of jealous insecurity, and I hated it. I'm typically not a jealous person. I'd like to think that I have a normal level of jealousy and self-esteem. But Jesus fucking Christ, I gotta follow a porn star?!? Who was funny and smart and hot?! Who broke his heart?! Whom he'd planned on spending an exciting life of sexual debauchery with before she abruptly ended it?! I don't care who you are or what you've been through in your life, that situation would make almost any woman feel like she wasn't good enough or sexual enough or pretty or adventurous enough. And— perhaps the toughest feeling to deal with—like she wasn't *woman* enough. After the first few torturous weeks, I finally came up with a word that accurately encapsulated how I felt: "femasculated."

A friend pointed out to me that this word has been used in the lesbian community under a different definition, but in this context, "femasculated" means feeling like you're never good enough as a woman, usually because of your outer appearance and usually in comparison to some other "ideal" woman. Like if your best friend was Kate Upton and she followed you around everywhere you went and she only wore a bikini and jogged in place and, yeah, she's super sweet and supportive and she loves you, but in the back of your mind you're anxious about everyone else's infatuation with her because those beautiful bouncing boobs are literally in your face at all times and she just won't go home! And now holidays are awkward because your male family members no longer care about the play you're in, and your doctor appointments suck—yeah, you have Lyme disease, but who cares? Just look at Kate Upton's bouncing titties and you'll be cured!!! My point is, Kate Upton's tits were not physically next to me at all times, but they were certainly in my *head* at all times. Only instead of images of bouncing tits it was images of Stephen having the time of his life boning the shit out of his highly sought after sex goddess of a girlfriend. Ex. Ex-girlfriend. I had to keep reminding myself of that.

The feelings of femasculation continued to grow as Stephen was trying to work through his heartache by telling *me* all the things he missed about her. That sure didn't help. Like, at all. In fact, that made my feelings ten times worse, but I was falling for him so I didn't voice my frustrations until it was too late. I knew all the things. *Way* too many things. Things I couldn't un-hear. Things that would keep me up at night and make me question what the fuck an unemployed aspiring comedian has to bring to the table that's more exciting than an award-winning, intelligent, dark-humored, beautiful porn star. There was one thing he told me in particular that I couldn't shake. We were walking to the subway from his apartment, talking our faces off like we always do, and he said, "Stoya used to take my hand and put it up her skirt, in public, to let me know how wet I made her." *Whoa. Uh. Okay. Cool. Do I gotta do that, or . . . ?* He later apologized for blurting that out, which was cool and all, but the image his words created in my head haunted me for years.

It gets better! And by better, I mean way worse. About six months into us dating, I started to notice that all the porn stores in New York (there are many) had a poster on their front door for this porn film called *Pirates*. Normally I would roast the shit out of a poster that ridiculous, but the only thing I could see as I walked by all those porn store doors was Stoya. Her eyes would follow me as I walked by, and (in my head) she would say things like, "Ha-ha! My pussy is better than yours! And I have an acting credit!" I never walked by more porn stores in my entire life than when I was at what I thought was the height of my femasculation days. Funny how that usually plays out. Then one day we were at Stephen's Brooklyn apartment and I suggested that he change his bedsheets because it had been a while. I don't know what it is about men and their disinterest in clean sheets and towels, but side note to all dudes: wash that shit more often! When I removed the fitted sheet from his mattress, I looked down and noticed an enormous circular stain. As if there had been a puddle that took up over half the bed. I really didn't want to know. But I also really wanted to know. "Stephen . . . what the fuck is that? Did you spill a gallon of iced tea on your bed or something?" "Oh. Um. Stoya. When she orgasms she kinda squirts everywhere, and . . ." "Aw, she does? That's great. No, no, really. Good for her. Squirts like a goddamn fire hydrant. Hey, could ya be a dear and *get a new motherfucking mattress pad, please*?!" (Cue newly realized feelings of inadequacy over lack of squirting.)

I finally expressed my concerns to Stephen, begging him to get another shoulder to cry on about his ex but trying incredibly hard not to clue him in to the fact that every cell in my body was oozing with insecurity and discomfort during these conversations. My efforts to cover up my lack of confidence often came out of my mouth as anger. Of *course* it did. Insecure people are usually the angriest, loudest kind of people. As Amber Rose told us during her episode of *Guys We Fucked,* "confidence is quiet and insecurity is loud." Well, mine was screaming from the top of a mountain through seventeen loudspeakers. The pedestal I had put Stoya on inside of my head was so tall that I couldn't see the top. Because it was covered by clouds. And if you took a plane to try to see the top of the pedestal, you'd soon find out that, *oh shit,* you're gonna need a rocket ship because that thing stretches into outer space!

This isn't something I'm dying to admit, but up until Stephen, I had always prided myself on being the hottest girl my current boyfriend had ever dated or, at the very least, in the top three. Now, whether or not that's actually true is up for discussion (because it probably isn't true—I was just being a shallow piece of shit). But regardless, it had given me comfort and confidence, which were now nowhere to be found. Because women in our society are mostly defined by what they look like. Because femininity has a very clear hierarchy of hotness, and we're constantly reminded of our place. We see it every day in magazines, on billboards, in television and movies. And it instills this false idea that our value as women is based, first and foremost, on how we look. I'm sure you've seen a straight couple walking down the street where the woman is a total babe and the guy is just kinda meh. You probably don't pay much attention to it. If anything, you think *He must be loaded.* Have you ever seen a couple where the man is mesmerizingly attractive and the woman is, by society's standards, just okay looking? And did it make you think *Whoa, wait a second. What the fuck is happening there? Can't . . . compute.* If you still don't know what I'm talking about, look at the comments section of literally any article online about Lena Dunham. It's some bullllllllll. Shit.

I worked to overcome my femasculation, mostly through healthy methods, including avoidance and denial. Just as I was starting to be semi-okay with the whole Stoya thing, it felt as if the universe said, "LOL JK. Go fuck yourself." I was walking to work when I passed one of those plastic newspaper kiosks with the latest issue of *The Village Voice* staring at me. Stoya's face was on the cover and the headline underneath read THE PRETTIEST GIRL IN NEW YORK IS A PORN STAR. I ripped my earbuds out of my ears, kicked the very sturdy kiosk with my very weak foot and yelled, *"Are you fucking kidding me with this shit?"* Luckily New York City has a large population of people roaming the sidewalks screaming to no one, so I blended in.

There was a period of time when my life felt like a nightmare fun house but when I looked in any of those warped mirrors, instead of seeing a wonky version of myself staring back at me, it was just Stoya. She was either chilling on the front door of a porn shop laughing and saying, "I'm better at sex than you!" or on literally any street corner in a *Village Voice* kiosk saying, "And I'm prettier than you!" But she wasn't actually saying any of that shit to me. *I* was. *I* put the words in her mouth and *I* yelled those words at myself. I was building her up in my head to be this huge bully and in a pathetic effort to feel in control, I'd think things like *You're not better than me, you're a fucking whore. You're just a sex worker.* Those thoughts made me feel like shit. That wasn't what I was about at *all* and the jealousy felt like a gross, cancerous sap that was covering my entire body. I desperately needed to change my approach, so I thought long and hard about all my insecurities and self-doubts. Then I scooped them up and I shoved them deep, deep down into a dark, black hole. *I know what I have to do*, I thought. *I gotta one-up this bitch.*

Don't ever try to one-up a porn star. It's not going to work out well.

The first time I went to the ER for a sex injury was right after Christmas of 2012. Stephen has always been an excellent gift giver, probably due to his disdain for meaningless bullshit. That Christmas, after I unwrapped an array of thoughtful gifts, he handed me a very heavy package that he said I couldn't open in front of my parents. I ripped the wrapping paper off and laid my eyes on the biggest dildo I had ever seen. At this point, my newly realized coping strategy had caused me to brag to Stephen about things I'd done sexually that I hadn't actually done. I glanced down at this dildo the size of Bigfoot's dick and said, "Oh, wow. That's a good size. We should use it this week!" As those words were leaving my mouth, I just thought to myself, *That's not gonna fit in there. That's not gonna fit anywhere.*

A few days later, back at his Brooklyn apartment, he proceeded to stick Bigfoot's cock into me. It was . . . different. I was mostly amazed that that monstrosity of a molded penis could make its way up there. Eventually, the dildo left, the intercourse took place, and we went to bed. At around 3 A.M. I woke up to sharp, heavy pain in my lower abdomen. Pains that make the worst period there could ever be pale in comparison. Something was very wrong, and I made Stephen drive me to the nearest hospital to figure out what the fuck it was. Much to my dismay, there was no female gynecologist on site during my visit, so a very reluctant older male doctor proceeded to give me a gynecological exam and inserted a freezing-cold, lube-coated wand up my vagina. Let the record show: that was the second time in five hours in which I'd had an unwanted object up me. Tears were falling down my face as I squeezed Stephen's hand and looked up to notice he was tearing up right along with me. It was an oddly beautiful bonding moment, but I would have settled for holding hands while running through a field of flowers any day over this bullshit. According to the doctor, I had an ovarian cyst that had burst. I made no mention of the dildo. No way in hell was I going to open up to an old man who'd just stuck his hands up me while wishing he was anywhere else in the world. I don't know if the dildo was the culprit, but if I had to guess, I'd say it played a part. Several follow-up appointments and one microscopic surgery later, I learned that I have cystic ovaries. My femasculation continued to go undiagnosed, which resulted in my second trip to the ER for a sex injury.

This visit was due to butt stuff gone awry. I was pretending to love anal sex and one afternoon, post-anal, I noticed I was bleeding heavily. Two hours later I noticed that, yep, I was still bleeding. I told Stephen and we were both alarmed, so after a few minutes of online searching, it was off to the ER! I was more up-front with the doctor this time around—she was a woman, so that made it easier. After a brief rectal exam, she concluded that I needed to eat more fiber, and I concluded that pretending to enjoy anal sex is stupid and expensive and can ruin your sheets and cut up your asshole.

That was the last time I had something inserted into my butt, but perhaps it won't be the last ever. I'm munching on dried bran flakes as I type this in hopes of one day getting back in the (anal) game. The thing is, I do enjoy anal sex. But on that day, prior to going to the ER, specifically during the anal sex, I felt an uncomfortable, painful sensation. No, it wasn't merely because there was a penis in my butt—it was different. I felt as if something wasn't right, and I failed to listen to my body over the fear of coming off as someone who wasn't down for anything in bed. It's so stupid looking back at it. I hate that I ignored my wonderful, precious body. That is the power of feeling femasculated.

But I haven't even gotten to the story of *peak* femasculation. Have you ever heard of a Fleshlight? If not, strap in! A Fleshlight is a sex toy for a person with a penis. On the outside, it looks like a giant, plastic flashlight. When you unscrew the cap and look inside, you will find a silicone vagina, butthole, or mouth, usually replicating those of a specific porn star. And who had one of the top-selling Fleshlights in the biz? Good ol' Stoya!! Before Stephen moved in with me, he owned about ten of Stoya's Fleshlights. One of the many stories he told me that I can't un-hear is that she used to ask him to test out the Fleshlights and give her feedback. I made him stop the story before he had the chance to give *me* the feedback, but I'm assuming it was great. I was well aware that he owned a bunch of these, but when he moved in with me, I asked him to throw them out and assumed he did just that. Isn't that the golden rule? You move on to a new girlfriend, you throw the old girlfriend's superskin vagina and butthole in the trash, right?

The day I discovered he kept one of those Fleshlights was the same day Hurricane Sandy battered the East Coast with record-breaking floods and power outages. Not thinking the storm was going to be that bad, I invited Corinne over to hang out. I figured we could make some funny comedy videos and write together. Little did she know she was about to witness the height of my femasculation era. During the peak of Hurricane Sandy, the basement level of our apartment started to flood with sewage water that made its way up through the toilet and bathtub. In a moment of panic, Corinne, Stephen, and I began taking as many things as we could carry upstairs, away from the poop water. I went to grab a box in Stephen's closet and paused for a moment. *What the hell is in this box?* Call it women's intuition, but I lifted the lid. "Oh, nice! A flashlight! We need that!" I unscrewed the cap, and much to my dismay, there was no light bulb. There was, however, a butthole! Stoya's butthole. Staring back at me, like she often did from movie posters and newspapers. Except this time it was her asshole. And all those insecurities I had shoved deep, deep down in that hole came bubbling up to the surface. I ran upstairs with her butthole in my left hand and I gave him the most lethal we're-gonna-talk-about-*this*-later look, so as not to make Corinne uncomfortable. I definitely still made her uncomfortable. She knew what was going on. No one wants to be present for another couple's fight. Especially when you're trapped in an apartment flooded with shit water and zero electricity. So we all pretended I didn't have the rage of a thousand suns inside me and everything was hunky-dory. Eventually we went to bed, Corinne on the couch and me, steaming, reluctantly lying next to a very concerned and uncomfortable Stephen. After Corinne returned to her light-filled, non-flooded apartment back in Harlem, Stephen and I had it out. I wouldn't even let him talk. I remember yelling, "You said you would throw these away! You were supposed to throw these away! Why did you keep this? What the fuck is wrong with you?" To which he replied, "I'm sorry! Look. I'm really sorry, but yes, I kept one, because I thought it was funny! I mean, how often do you date someone with a bestselling butthole?" That's when I realized he was over her. I wasn't. We had always talked about having her on the podcast, but in the past, I would always say some sideways comment about her under my breath and he'd change his mind, rightfully so. But at the end of our fight, I said, "*Oh, we're interviewing her.*" And that's when everything I had been feeling for the past four years finally came to a head.

I'll never forget the moments outside our recording studio as I waited for her to arrive, chain-smoking and shaking with nervousness. I never wanted Stephen to know how insecure she made me feel, and I certainly didn't want *her* to know. She'd have power over me. She'd win. She'd be the better, hotter, dreamier, cooler girlfriend and I'd be some sad sack of shit whining in a corner asking strangers if they think I'm pretty. When I spotted her walking down the block, I panicked, but I don't think she could tell. She greeted me with a warm smile, gave me a hug, and said, "Hey! This is the weirdest day ever, right?!" and all the feelings that had been building up for four years started to melt away.

The podcast interview was enjoyable, intriguing, insightful, and exactly what I needed in order to humanize her. After over an hour of porn-related sex questions, I very hesitantly admitted my insecurities toward her, which she handled with great care and understanding. She told me all about people she encounters on a day-to-day basis who think they know her and treat her like a second-class citizen because of it. She told me about the time a landlord wanted an entire year's rent up front after she disclosed what she did for work on her lease application. Sometimes strange men approach her in public and say something repulsive or proposition her for sex. She gets slut-shamed constantly. Then she said something that made my heart sink. She said, "It feels like I'm standing on top of a pedestal *inside of a garbage can*." That hit me like a ton of bricks and I realized, *Shit . . . I'm part of the garbage can*. After that day, I felt as if a thousand pounds of weight had been lifted off my shoulders and I had learned an important, life-changing lesson. That lesson is this: In terms of how I treat myself and how I treat other women, I don't want to add to the garbage. I want to be the pedestal.

If you're a woman reading this right now, think back and ask yourself if there was ever a moment when you said or thought "Ugh, she's such a slut." If there was, I guarantee it was because that woman made you feel like *you* weren't woman enough or sexual enough or hot enough. Feeling femasculated can turn you into a raging asshole. Not the post-anal, bleeding kind. The ugly, mean-girl kind. No ER doctor can help you with that. You need to fix it on your own by asking yourself the questions you've been avoiding and by putting your big-girl pants on and dealing with your feelings instead of shoving them down into a dark place. From the bottom of my heart, I beg you . . . save yourself the trouble and do it before you end up getting microscopic surgery or a rectal exam. Do it before you end up holding someone's superskin butthole in your hand as your apartment floods with poop water and your expensive desk chair gets ruined because you were too busy being angry to run it upstairs. Do it before those feelings turn you into an ugly, cruel version of who you really are.

UR So Gay

CORINNE

Men are the product of a culture that does not tolerate weakness in any form. And somehow homosexuality has kind of been branded as a form of weakness in that the members of its community are stereotypically more feminine (and we just can't have that, can we?). This creates a complex and confusing relationship to our sexuality, especially if our sexuality is celebrated with parades but also hidden from the Boy Scouts. When the news first broke of the shooting at gay nightclub Pulse in Orlando, it seemed as if it was an act of terror. You know, like ISIS terror. The brand of terror we as humans in the twenty-first century have become all too familiar with. As the story unraveled, however, we learned it was a terror much deeper than that. Yes, the gunman did pledge allegiance to ISIS, but was that just to deflect from the deeply personal reasons he felt the need to take the lives of so many people living proudly and joyously in the LGBTQ+ community? After all, in the words of psychiatrist James Gilligan, "All violence is an attempt to replace shame with self-esteem."* The gunman's ex-wife assured us after the massacre that while, yes, this man was brutal and violent and filled with hate . . . a lot of that hate started from within because he was gay and that was not okay with his religion or his family, namely his father. In a Facebook status update

---

* Jon Ronson, *So You've Been Publicly Shamed* (New York: Riverhead Books, 2015).

about the incident made by gay author and former podcast guest David Crabb, he notes that "[i]t's strange how quickly this murderer's father came forward to reject knowledge of terrorist connections but was sure to stress how much his son hated gay people. *He hated them.* And here we are . . . with news that the killer had been going to the club for three years, he'd asked men on dates, had gay dating apps on his phone . . . And now his ex-wife is speaking openly about his father screaming at him for being gay right in front of her. It's sad and disheartening and reminds me how lucky I am not to have come from a family and a culture like this man."

While I've certainly had lots of face time (and dick time) with men, both hetero and homosexual, I am not one myself (gender may be fluid, but honestly I just identify as a boring ol' female—please respect that too), so I plucked the mind of my boyfriend, James, a bit to get his thoughts on the subject since he's one of the most stereotypically masculine people I know. He told me that he feels no pressure to stifle his emotions and, rather, thinks it's necessary for him to remain somewhat stoic, as it aids in the ebb and flow of the world. He said, with no uncertainty, people "look to males for support and guidance," and because we've "fucked with gender roles, relationships aren't working out anymore." While James's reply didn't necessarily match the angle I was trying for, I think it's more important to print his true response rather than to cater to my own agenda.

James, like me, is not always the best communicator, a common "problem" with men. But is this "progressive" notion accurate that men's right to feel all the feels has been stolen from them or has modern society just decided to play God like we have historically done time and time again? Is it more convenient for us women to assume that all the guys in our life are repressed so we don't feel bad about ourselves if we don't get the gushy treatment we sometimes want?

In *Social Psychology and Human Nature,* Roy F. Baumeister and Brad J. Bushman argue that men may actually find it harder to calm their emotions down than women, and so they tend to attempt avoiding emotion. This presents a bit of a different concept from what mainstream liberalism would have us believe. Men aren't masking their emotions as a reaction to society but as a most basic part of humanity: self-preservation. Baumeister and Bushman's text goes on to share that "[t]his pattern appears to be maintained in marital interactions: When married couples argue, husbands show stronger and longer-lasting physiological arousal than wives." Furthermore, women self-report having more empathy than men, "but when research uses objective measures of understanding the emotional states of others, no gender difference is found." And possibly most stirring of all: "When a love relationship breaks up, men suffer more intense emotional distress than women."*

After some thought, I realized James's commentary on his gender role was almost identical to another radical thinker who was arguably one of the most polarizing guests on *Guys We Fucked*—comedian, former pimp, and host of *The Beige Phillip Show* Dante Nero. The relationship advice Nero gives on his (very popular) show is entirely based on getting back into traditional gender roles because, while they might feel archaic at times, that's how things were meant to be. While I've spent the past year and a half assuming that James would love to be "allowed" to be more emotional and that military school must've

---

* Roy F. Baumeister and Brad J. Bushman, *Social Psychology and Human Nature, 2nd edition* (Belmont, CA: Wadsworth, Cengage Learning, 2009), 186, https://books.google.com/books?id=pTw4IMrOg0sC&pg=PA186&lpg=PA186&dq=are+men+actually+stifling+their+emotion&source=bl&ots=N1ZZFrA7Yj&sig=7675YUCuBMvlLGbF_IAPQ4MhCio&hl=en&sa=X&ved=0ahUKEwjYrbua8-PTAhWBKiYKHb50C60Q6AEIODAD#v=onepage&q=are%20men%20actually%20stifling%20their%20emotion&f=false.

scared all the sensitivities out of him, he just informed me it actually taught him the discipline he was lacking, helped him make friends and feel more confident, and got him away from a toxic post-divorce home environment with two families who hated each other. And he even cries from time to time, like to mourn a breakup or when he recently got scary health news about his mother. So while I'm sure some men are repressed emotionally—as are members of all genders—this metaphorical plastic bag that we speculate is suffocating all of male kind might not actually exist. As with most issues, the burden of being a man might be just as elaborate as the burden of being a woman.

Fat boy confidence in hotty body

...ed Nipple Shame?

Stretchy balls

He...

Depression, Gay, 14 and 200 pounds

...ituary (Odicktuary???)

Did I handle this blowjob the right way?

I saw a micro penis

Licking a strangers butthole

...ctile dysfunction, ...all dicks & squirting

My IUD Pokes Penises

Anxiety is my vaginas worst enemy

...ockblock

Big boob-ed Italian Jew - Are they using me for my titties?

Your pussy will be mangled after gangbang!

DO NOT USE WARMING LUBE DURING ANAL SEX

...issues are affecting ...with sex

thank you for addressing the butt crack hair! (seriously)

Tick tock says his cock... Every god damn morning.

My body, My ch...

Asses, Tits, and Ge...

anxiety = no boner

I broke my ex boyfriends dick once...

...you can have an orgasm ...ut the vaginal contractions?

BOYFRIEND HATES HIS BODY

teachers can't show their tits ?

resending you my hairy vag poem cos of bad formatting

Corinne's Butt

Smalllllllll Penis

My Sister's Future Boob Job

To all those who's bodies and mind have become a lost home.

I was fired for being too fat.

18, Fat, Ugly and Never Been Kissed

...ad an orgasm

Talkin' about body positivity / size / fat shaming / being a giant

WHY ...HIM

My girlfriend learned how to have vaginal orgasms and you can too! (I think)

An easy (and ...to get your g...

Pubic Hair - Use a Beard Trimmer

...n orgasm ...ontractions?

MY BEST FRIEND THINKS I'M A FAT SLUT??????

Has the military created my body issues or is this all my fault?

I wanna be a horny bitch but m... body is betraying me!!! SOS!!!!

My girlfriend Hates her body :(

...tion: Body Hair... self ...cious, yes or no?... ...ghts?..

No one told me I could get HERPES on my face

IT TOOK ME 21 YEARS TO ORGASM

I vomited

...ex boyfriends dick?

I throw up when I swallow cum

Lots of sex, no orgas...

...his dick made me puke

I GOT WET SITTING NEXT TO A GUY?!

Came so hard I pooped

Peri...

Do transwomen have balls??

hi I also have mom issues how are you

skinny shaming is okay, right?...

Fat girl too confident for a fat guy??

Am I just a body double?

...at??

Fanboy praise, learning to be a feminist father and body-shaming

My boyfriend wants a dick in his ass

Dick so good I crie...

Girls Who Love Balls

Curvy girl with fat problems/never orgasmed before with a dude..

...e aftermath ...eding

I'm 20 and my tits are already sagging.

Flax seeds on my

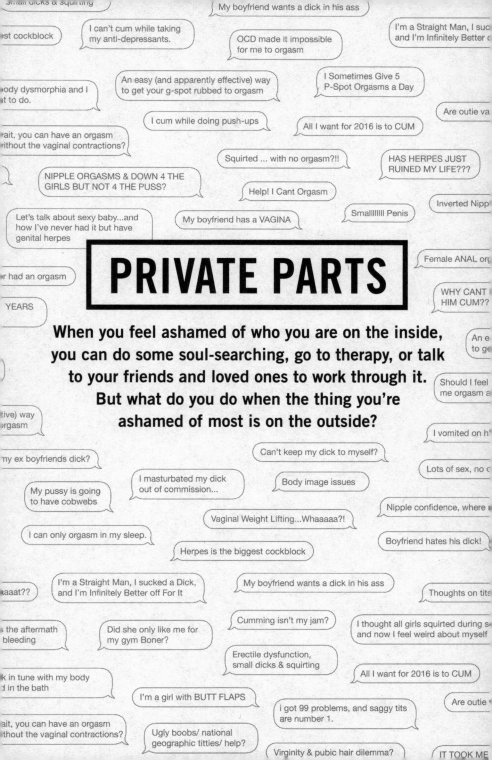

small dicks & squirting

My boyfriend wants a dick in his ass

I can't cum while taking my anti-depressants.

st cockblock

I'm a Straight Man, I suc and I'm Infinitely Better o

OCD made it impossible for me to orgasm

ody dysmorphia and I t to do.

An easy (and apparently effective) way to get your g-spot rubbed to orgasm

I Sometimes Give 5 P-Spot Orgasms a Day

Are outie va

I cum while doing push-ups

All I want for 2016 is to CUM

ait, you can have an orgasm ithout the vaginal contractions?

Squirted ... with no orgasm?!!

HAS HERPES JUST RUINED MY LIFE???

NIPPLE ORGASMS & DOWN 4 THE GIRLS BUT NOT 4 THE PUSS?

Help! I Cant Orgasm

Inverted Nipp

Let's talk about sexy baby...and how I've never had it but have genital herpes

My boyfriend has a VAGINA

Smalllllll Penis

Female ANAL or

r had an orgasm

PRIVATE PARTS

WHY CANT HIM CUM??

YEARS

When you feel ashamed of who you are on the inside, you can do some soul-searching, go to therapy, or talk to your friends and loved ones to work through it. But what do you do when the thing you're ashamed of most is on the outside?

An e to ge

Should I feel me orgasm a

tive) way rgasm

I vomited on h'

my ex boyfriends dick?

Can't keep my dick to myself?

Lots of sex, no c

I masturbated my dick out of commission...

Body image issues

My pussy is going to have cobwebs

Nipple confidence, where

Vaginal Weight Lifting...Whaaaaa?!

I can only orgasm in my sleep.

Boyfriend hates his dick!

Herpes is the biggest cockblock

aaaat??

I'm a Straight Man, I sucked a Dick, and I'm Infinitely Better off For It

My boyfriend wants a dick in his ass

Thoughts on tits

s the aftermath bleeding

Did she only like me for my gym Boner?

Cumming isn't my jam?

I thought all girls squirted during s and now I feel weird about myself

Erectile dysfunction, small dicks & squirting

k in tune with my body d in the bath

All I want for 2016 is to CUM

I'm a girl with BUTT FLAPS

Are outie

ait, you can have an orgasm ithout the vaginal contractions?

Ugly boobs/ national geographic titties/ help?

i got 99 problems, and saggy tits are number 1.

Virginity & pubic hair dilemma?

IT TOOK ME

Vaginas

PUSSIES/COOTERS/LOVE TACOS/ PUNANI/PENIS FLY TRAPS/ETC.

Krystyna

Vaginas are complicated. If you have one, you know this. If you don't have one but you've been face-to-face with one, you might have felt equal parts fascination and perplexity. Vaginas make the world go 'round. They can be used as currency. They can strike fear in societies for centuries. They're the reason a lot of straight guys step foot in bars. They've inspired dramatic monologues. And I'm willing to bet they've started a shit ton of wars.

Let's start with the basics. Contrary to what you may have seen in porn, vaginas vary in size, shape, color, width, length, height, and ability to crush penises with their razor-sharp teeth (JK, I wish). The more I read up on anatomy, the more I come to terms with the fact that I don't know jack shit about my own body. Shout-out to public sex education and parents who avoid talking about anatomy with their kids!

Like a lot of young women, I was inspired to hold a mirror up to my vagina in order to get a good look after I watched the episode of *Sex and the City* in which Samantha shames Charlotte into doing the same. What varies the most amongst vaginas are the labia, the folds of skin on either side of the vaginal opening. The porn industry would have you believe that all labia on the planet are neatly tucked in, like a cute little puppy wrapped in a warm blanket on a snowy afternoon. Nope. No. No. No, a thousand times no. Let's get that idea out of our heads immediately. Some countries (*cough* Australia *cough*) have made it *illegal* to show a woman's vagina in pornography magazines unless it's the cute little puppy kind. In which case, show the world, girl! You won the pussy lottery! They go so far as to hire people (men) whose sole job is to sit at a computer all day and Photoshop labia so they appear nice and tucked. This is exactly why labiaplasty surgeries are so common in countries like Australia. To its credit, the Royal Australian College of General Practitioners has issued guidelines for referring women to see a specialist for labiaplasty. One of the guidelines requires doctors to show women all the different types of labia, in case the women think their labia are a disgusting monstrosity undeserving of love, only to discover that they all look like asymmetrical alien elephant ears. Sure enough, this decreased labiaplasty procedures by 28 percent. But we're forgetting a very important facet to all this: *Why the fuck is there a cosmetic surgery for vaginas that are perfectly normal and healthy!?!?!*

For your reference, here are illustrations of some labia, each unique as fuck. This isn't every single type of labia that exists in the world, but it gives you a good idea of the variety:

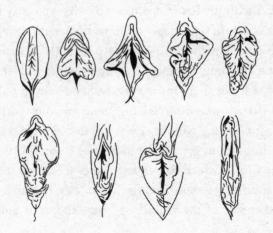

You see that, people!? Labia come in all styles. None is better or worse than the next, and if you think otherwise, congratulations! You've been brainwashed by self-destructive societal bullshit and it's preventing you from living your life to the fullest and enjoying the wonderments of masturbation and sex. Now stop being silly and learn to love what you've got. Or what you're fortunate enough to encounter.

The Vagina Dialogues, or My Pussy Is Screaming

I have one of those tucked-in *Playboy* vaginas that the old men in the Australian law-making body seem to be so precious about. I've always liked my vagina, but not because of how it looks. I mean, it's all I've ever known down there. I've looked at my vagina up close in a mirror countless times. Some instances were purely out of curiosity, others were to investigate the pubic hair situation, and a few personal examinations were made holding my breath and saying a prayer that the unbearable itchiness wasn't accompanied by crazy bumps or growths or whatever the fuck can happen when you contract an STI. You wouldn't guess it by the title of our podcast, but I've never contracted an STI. This is brought to you purely by luck, considering all the condomless sex I so stupidly initiated in my early twenties. I know men and women who have contracted everything from chlamydia to herpes yet have had sex only one or two times. The worst thing that's ever happened to my vaginal area is Brian Gr—just kidding—is a yeast infection. I've had plenty of those, but the most recent one lasted almost a month and itched so fucking badly that I couldn't sleep. I've put hot water on it. I've put ice in it. I've tried all the creams. I've taken all the baths. If you've gotten this far and you're unsure what a yeast infection is, (1) good for you, and (2) it's when too many yeast cells are growing in the vagina. All vaginas have these cells in addition to bacteria that are there to keep the yeast under control. If there's an imbalance in your system, the bacteria are all like "Oh shit, too much! Too much!" and the yeast cells take over. This can happen for many different reasons. You pregnant? Yeast infection. You got diabetes? Yeast infection. You stressed? Yeast infection. You tired as hell cause you didn't get a lot of sleep this past week? Yeast infection. You eatin' a lot of sugary shit? Yeast infection. Some women can do all of the aforementioned activities and never get a yeast infection, and to those women I say, "Good for you. No, seriously, I'm happy for you." And don't get me started on urinary tract infections.

Okay, you got me started. I've been hospitalized for those a bunch. If you don't know about UTIs, again, congratulations—you've never had one and you've never been close with a person who has, because if you did, you'd know about it. A UTI affects all the parts of the body involved in urination. This includes the kidneys, bladder, ureters (tubes that drain urine from the kidneys), and urethra. It can also negatively affect the comfort you typically enjoy while doing things like sitting. And standing. And walking. And having sex. And being awake in general. You can get a UTI if certain bacteria from your butthole, such as *E. coli*, come into contact with your urethra. These bacteria can make their way to your urethra in several ways, including wiping back to front, if you're a woman, or just having vigorous sex in general. UTIs can happen to both men and women, but much like lupus, stalkers, sexually transmitted infections, the wage gap, celiac disease, acne, Alzheimer's, and the likelihood of getting murdered by an ex-lover, they affect women way more. On average, 40 percent of vagina owners will contract a urinary tract infection at least once in their lives, compared to 12 percent of penis havers. Awesome!

If a UTI goes unnoticed, it can spread to your kidneys and land you in the hospital with loads of lower back pain and a fever. The first time this happened to me, I was sixteen and on my period. When you go to the ER for a UTI while on your period, the nurse does this really fun thing where she sticks a catheter up your urethra and you scream-cry while holding your mom's hand. Antibiotics will usually clear it up fast, but most doctors need a clean, period-blood-free urine sample to verify that it is in fact a UTI.

Despite my trials and tribulations, I'm still incredibly appreciative of my vagina. It's been my friend when I'm stressed out. When I look in the mirror, depending on the angle, it kind of looks like it's smiling back at me, which is weird but fun. However, if I could change one thing about my vagina, it would probably be my ability to orgasm the way I've heard other women say they orgasm. After talking about pussies on a podcast for three years, it has come to my attention that some women cum often and in more places with much less stimulation required than I. One past guest told me that she can have clitoral and vaginal orgasms all day and all night from *just* a penis being inside her. That's it. A penis. Nothing else. Several studies suggest that it has to do with your anatomy and the size of your clitoris, as well as its distance from your urethra and vaginal opening. I tend to think it has more to do with having a magical vagina and would love to know what a gal has to do to get one of those.

Penises

DICKS/COCKS/BALD-HEADED YOGURT SLINGERS/WANGS/WEENERS/ETC.

Krystyna

Corinne and I recently performed in Boston and had a killer show with a lively audience that was very into coming on stage and sharing their sexcapades with us. After every show we do a meet and greet, and toward the end of that show, a group of women and one guy came up to us. The guy didn't want to get in the photo, but afterward, when we said thank you for coming, he came up close to me and whispered, "Please be honest . . . Does size matter?" By his eager but sincere tone, I could tell he didn't want me to bullshit him, and I respect that. However, there was a line of people behind him waiting, and my parents happened to be sitting three feet away from me, taking photos of us saying hello to fans, so I kept it short and sweet: "As long as you know what you're doing in other departments, no." He seemed relieved.

But now that I'm not in a rush and can expand on this, me saying that penis size does not matter whatsoever is not entirely true. I hesitate to write that sentence down in a book about dispelling sexual shame because I don't want to make a guy feel bad about what he's got, but I'd be a much bigger asshole if I lied. Size does matter. And if you have a small penis, it matters that you step up your game in other areas. It feels like women get shamed for every goddamn limb and hole on their body, but when it comes to sexual pleasure, I want my partner to be able to tell me if I'm not satisfying him, and I'm going to want some feedback so that I can change whatever it is I'm doing. It takes a few tries to leave your ego out of this type of conversation, but you can't get mad if someone is merely being honest with you. If you prioritize a woman's pleasure (or a man's, for all the gay and bi dudes), and you get off on making her (him, they, etc.) cum, I don't give a shit what is attached to you. I've encountered a cornucopia of penises in my life, and all but one have been enjoyable to gaze at, lick, touch, and feel inside me. The one dick that didn't tickle my fancy was more about the guy himself, because he didn't know his way around a woman's body and had no sense of rhythm, which had nothing to do with the size of his penis. *But!* He did happen to have the smallest penis of any guy I've slept with, so I think his lack of skill was directly correlated to his self-confidence in the bedroom. If you aren't packing, I can think of plenty of ways to enjoy sex with you that have nothing to do with your dick, but you have to have some sense of rhythm and dexterity with your tongue and hands or at least a willingness to learn.

Men are more than the size and shape of their penises, and I gotta say, women can be heartless about this subject, as if men are incapable of feeling insecure about themselves. This couldn't be further from the truth. If a sexual relationship involves a penis getting hard in order to do the thing you want to do, that's a lot of fucking pressure to perform. Of course there are alternative solutions to this problem, but the mental weight and shame that can follow a flaccid dick isn't easy to come to terms with. I've been with several guys who couldn't get it up, and by now I've realized it has nothing to do with me not being attractive enough. The one guy who comes to mind when I think of dicks that just wouldn't get hard is the only guy I fucked who I met at a bar. He was so attractive, holy shit. Tall, shaved head, blueish-green eyes. Jacked as *fuck*. We "slept" together maybe four times, and every time he was trying to shove his flaccid penis inside me without ever acknowledging that, hey, maybe that's not gonna work out right now. I never said anything because part of me wanted to see how far he would go before addressing it. It was the worst game of Russian roulette ever. Finally he told me he does a ton of blow and his dick never works when he's on it. "So . . . uh . . . how about you don't snort drugs before you invite me back to your place? *Or* eat me out instead! There's a crazy idea!" I ended it with him after that conversation, over both his unwillingness to not do cocaine and the confused look on his face when I asked him to eat me out.

Another fun fact I've learned about dicks is this: just because a guy cums early doesn't mean you're the hottest person he's ever been inside of. It's nice to think that, so no harm if you do, but you should know that your hotness is simply not a factor during minute-man encounters. I've talked to every guy I'm friends with about this because I honestly didn't believe it was true at first. Some friends also explained to me that sometimes they can't get it up the first few times they sleep with someone new. This has everything to do with performance anxiety and nothing to do with how attracted they are to their partner. See? Penises can be complex too!

They come in all varieties, just like vaginas—small, large, curved, circumcised, uncircumcised, thick, thin. You never know what you're gonna get before those pants come off. It's an exciting gamble, for the most part!

CORINNE

Nitpicking Our Bodies

Your vagina smells. And it's pretty loose. Your face is a mess. You look tired. And pale. And old. Cover your lips. And your eyes. And your cheeks. Actually, while you're at it, can you just put a coat of paint over your whole fucking face? But not like "too much." You still want to look natural. And let's not even talk about your hair. Please straighten that, you monster. But, like, still have it maintain a good amount of volume, okay? Wait, wait, wait, are you trying to walk out of the house without your leg makeup on? Also, you look fat. Have you eaten today? How. Dare. You . . . And voilà, that's how the beauty industry magically pulls shame out of thin air!

I feel like at least once a week I find something new on my body that apparently I should feel bad about. For instance, I've had a "beefy" vagina all my life. I never thought anything of it until I was twenty-nine years old and learned about labiaplasty. This procedure can actually be physically harmful and desensitize the pussy during sex. It also creates the idea that if your vagina doesn't look a particular way, there is something wrong. And, c'mon, no one wants to think something is wrong, even cosmetically, with their vagina. (Although, if you snuck a peak at the photos section on my phone, you would very quickly realize I'm perhaps a little too cool with mine.)

Very simply, insecurity breeds shame, which equals money. And for a very long time we have let big business profit off our self-worth.

People are putting dinner on the table for their families by promising to fix things on our bodies that weren't broken in the first place. These products and procedures put the same doubt into our minds that Regis Philbin planted every time he asked a *Who Wants to Be a Millionaire?* contestant "Is that your final answer?"

On the "Shame—What Is It?" episode of her podcast *How She Really Does It*, Koren Motekaitis explains that women register shame when it comes to "unattainable, conflicting, competing expectations" about who they're supposed to be, which quickly becomes a straightjacket, whereas men register shame as weakness. For women, Motekaitis points out, "perfection is the birthplace of shame" because it "shields your heart from being hurt." And what is it to be a woman, after all, if not a constant struggle of keeping your head above the waters of imperfection? We are certainly not born with this need to be perfect; that is something instilled in us from a young (and getting younger) age. It's hard not to buy a waist trainer (which is just us bringing back the medieval corset, if you hadn't noticed) or to try that new detox tea cleanse when you're surrounded by images of women—on your favorite TV show, winning Miss America, selling tampons, and getting the guy—who are skinny, pretty much always white, and often have big boobs. The more we see someone else's version of perfection, the harder it gets to maintain a sense of what would *feel perfect for us*.

How did we even learn what cankles are? How did we decide that a muffin top was unacceptable? Why are we comparing our bodies to baked goods? Every woman's body has value, and yet we sometimes appraise our bodies at less than zero. Your body is not a stock. There is no multiple ownership. There is a sole proprietor and it is you. So while it's fine to enjoy Instagram models as the filtered art they are, we have to stop letting the images companies pump into our minds about women dictate how we feel about ourselves. Remember, the state of women's bodies and our perception of ourselves is all a money game. The next time you look in the mirror and don't like what you see, take a second and think about if the problem is not liking what you see or what you see not matching up with what you have been taught to like. Yes, I think it's a woman's choice and right to get aesthetic surgery, but keep in mind that the "perfect woman" image is just something else created by corporations so they can profit off you, similar to how Joe Camel helped convince a lot of people that smoking greatly escalates your level of cool. The media *creates insecurities* and then the beauty industry creates products to help you deal with those insecurities. And men only judge you based on these things because that's what they are taught. They are told what type of woman they are supposed to like, even if what they truly want is a full-bellied goddess (who is probably much more fun to be with than the chick on the tea cleanse).

Remember: being unique has the most value. When being pretty is not what's important, you end up feeling both pretty *and* important.

ake Me Sick?

Condoms suck!!

in having anal sex with me?

Thinking about other woman during sex?

lly want

Dick so good I cried

Sometimes painful sex isn't an STD or a really big penis

HELP ME PUT STUFF MY BOYFRIEND'S BU

ped to threesomes: story

My friend won't stop showing me her boobs

I can only cum when I'm asleep, I'm a girl

Am I a Bad Fe Wanting To Ea

FART FETISH

How to teach a man to do me right

''LET ME JUST MAKE YOU CUM REAL QUICK"

Gang Bang

My boss thought I was jerking off on company time.

Ass licking- woman to man

-worker Found My Butt Should We Talk About It

I tried getting laid for three days and all I got was pissed on and some soft dicks

What do you do when a guy rubs his boner on you?

The woma had sex w peed on c her over a

yfriend had an orgy was sleeping.

Is he faking it? Does he not know what it means to cum?

SKINNY DRUNK AND HORNY

Where Do You Guys Stand On Selling Your Body?

ays his cock… damn morning.

Butt Sex?

my orgasm is smaller than your dick!!!! (a novel by me)

Gethard

To Jerk off in a relationship or not to jerk off.

shower head

Orgasm so good I weant deaf for a couple of minutes

started fucking in Disney World, where did the magic go

I'M AFRAID TO BOYFRIENDS

G??

I WAS SUCKING DICK WRONG TOO, KRYSTYNA

Butt stuff and dude-dude threesomes

ist for Not ussy?

Ass eating - HELP

I can take a load on my face AND raise your kids

Attached is the aftermath of my dick bleeding

hts in 1

I had a threesome with my wife and another man

Eat gravy out of my girlfriends pussy?

or kink for room

Hey so my boyfriend surprised butt-plugged me!!

My boyfriend told me to put my finger in his ass and now he won't talk

I'm a slut leader sex St Louis! hosting orgi dick, making dreams

This asshole won't go down!

My Life Story & Dying to be Tag Teamed

Husband Watched Me Fuck Mailman

Just bought a fake dick and still can't cum???

husband eekend uld I invite

I'm Afraid My Vagina Might Be Cursed

SHE WANTS HER FRIEND TO TWERK ON MY DICK?

I MASTURBAT FRIEND. And

Tips on How to Finger my Boyfriend's Ass??

Make America HARD Again

True Life: Living in a cum desert.

nd to ssy!

Epic deep-throat story gone hilariously awry

Abortions and boys and

I want my boyfriend to eat my friend's pussy!

Did Cum or Pizza Make Me Sick?

How can i trick my boyfriend in having anal sex with me?

Am I sexually turned on by my dead sibling?

"I love you but I really want to eat some pussy"

We had an accidental 3some with our dog

I masturbated my dick out of commission...

From gang raped to threesomes: my Cinderella story

Where all the hot swingers at?

Guys won't cum on my face

MY EX HAD A FART FETISH

My husband gives me stability, but my side dick makes me squirt.

I cannot make my chick cum.

ction: It takes 6 to Gang Bang

The boy who couldn't cum

I lost my virginity in

i have no idea what I'm doing when it comes to anal

Gay porn for straight men

husband eekend uld I invite

HELP! I JUST CAUGHT MY BOYFRIEND JERKING OFF IN MY CAR!!!

I Fist My Girlfriend Regula

My boyfriend had an orgy while I was sleeping.

The humour behind jobs. Is there any?

SEXUAL ACTS

Am I a Bad Wanting To

hinking about other woman during sex?

Threesome with husband and ex?

Strip uno, almost threesomes, Amsterdam and the time my brother got my sloppy seconds

Masturbating with a shower head

WON'T BE ABLE TO GIVE BLOW JOBS FOR MONTHS

OMES AND SQUIRTING??

I just masturbated, and felt moved to write a thank you letter

Eating Pussy Is Ruining My Sex Life

Am I a Bad Feminist for Not Wanting To Eat Pussy?

SOS!!! 24 YEAR OLD GUY ABOUT TO HAVE HIS FIRST THREESOME!!!!

THE BITCH'S BOYFRI GREEDY IN OUR THR

Threesomes and Sex with Bosses HOT Son???

My Kink Is Breaking My Heart

I have the female equivalent of blue balls

How Do You Threesome? #unicorndreams

Clusterfuck of confusion on pursuing kink fantasies/profession

guy has a major kink for lay in the bedroom

threeway for my boyfriend?

I rediscovered comedy but first put a finger up my boyfriend's arse crack – thank you!

I CANT STOP MASTURBATING AT WORK!

Possible to live happily ev one dick? PLEASE HELP!

BEST

MONSTER DICK MADE ME BLEED

Krystyna, how do you lick da booty hole? Like logistically...

My boyfriend refuse sleep with me

The woman me and my husband had sex with over the weekend

sucking dick or

CORINNE

Masturbation

A TUG AS OLD AS TIME

Although masturbation has certainly evolved over the centuries, it's actually one of the world's oldest pastimes—depictions of both male and female masturbation can be found in prehistoric rock paintings around the world. The ancient Greeks acknowledged it as a healthy tool to prevent sexual frustration and credited the Greek god Hermes with inventing it as a way to keep his son from suffering unrequited feelings for a woman. Ancient Egyptians thought it to be truly magical when performed by a god and believed Atum created the universe by masturbating until he came. And the ancient Romans consistently used it as a theme in Latin satire. In fact, there is talk of masturbation in every historic culture except for five small ethnic groups in Africa's Congo Basin, who even today are confused by the mere concept and don't have a word in their languages for the practice.

Throughout human history masturbation has been not only talked about at length but also talked about *positively*. In fact, it wasn't until the early 1700s that anyone even uttered a negative word about masturbation. Bored and obviously not getting any dick or pussy, an anonymous religious physician wrote and distributed a pamphlet throughout London entitled *Onania: or, The Heinous Sin of Self-Pollution, and All*

Its Frightful Consequences (in Both Sexes) Considered: With Spiritual and Physical Advice to Those Who Have Already Injured Themselves by This Abominable Practice. Not only was the title a bit wordy and over-dramatic; it was also a ploy for the doctor to sell his "strengthening tincture" and "prolific powder." Perhaps this was when the concept of profiting from convincing people something is wrong with them was born. It was all downhill from here, and many men considered to be intelligent hopped on board the no self-pleasure train: British physician Robert James called it an "incurable disorder" in his *A Medicinal Dictionary;* Swiss physician Samuel-Auguste-David Tissot published *L'Onanisme* in 1760, claiming masturbation could cause reduction of memory and reason, gout, and rheumatism; in 1812 Benjamin Rush, a Founding Father of the United States, cited masturbation as a cause for several types of mental illness in *Medical Inquiries and Observations upon the Diseases of the Mind;* in 1838 psychiatrist Etienne Esquirol stated it was "recognized in all countries as a cause of insanity" in *Des Maladies Mentales;* and as recently as the 1990s Abd al-Aziz bin Baz, the Grand Mufti of Saudi Arabia, claimed masturbation disrupted the digestive system and did damage to the spine. Oh, and bad news if you've ever eaten corn flakes or graham crackers—those were invented by Doctor John Harvey Kellogg and inspired by Reverend Sylvester Graham, respectively, who both promoted a masturbation remedy that included a bland vegetarian diet. Even great philosophers like Immanuel Kant and Jean-Jacques Rousseau considered the practice immoral and akin to mental rape. Oof. And Boy Scouts? That was actually an organization founded to distract boys from tugging at their own dicks. The mastermind behind The Scout Association, Robert Baden-Powell, suggested that young boys should involve themselves with physical activity so they would become too tired to stick their dicks in apple pie. Ya gotta hand it to the dude. He really didn't want lads fapping.

Then along came Alfred Kinsey, who throughout the 1940s and 1950s was like "Um, basically everyone in America is masturbating, guys. It's . . . natural." And whaddya know? In 1972 the American Medical Association declared it as normal. Big of them. But things weren't okay just yet, because in 1994 U.S. Surgeon General Jocelyn Elders mentioned in passing that masturbation should be talked about in schools as safe and healthy, and she was forced to resign because a bunch of morons reinterpreted her words and claimed she wanted teachers to educate kids on how to get themselves off (which if done with a bit of finesse isn't really such a bad fucking idea). As a graduate of the public school system, I can confidently state that at no point in my life have I needed to know how to play kickball, steal the bacon, or write in cursive, but had I known how to make myself cum before college, when my boyfriend had to take time away from collecting obscure WWE action figures to teach me, I would've been a lot less "hysterical" about the fact that Dane Cook did not feel the same way about me as I felt about him. Or even know I existed.

So to save you all from the misery of depending on someone else to bring your genitals pleasure, we want to shove masturbation out of the shadows and give you the facts about self-pleasure so you can paddle your pink canoe or beat your meat without feeling like a freak.

Krystyna

The Art of Jerking Off

I first started masturbating when I was around eight or nine years old. All I knew about masturbating was that it was a thing that felt *real* good and it might make me pregnant. Every time I went to pee during the early hump era, I would frantically examine the toilet paper for any signs of blood because that meant I was pregnant with triplets probably. I was terrified, but did it stop me? Not a chance.

By the age of six or seven, most children have discovered their genitals and the fun that can be had by playing with them. It's completely normal for a kid that young to be masturbating, and for the love of god, don't shame them if you happen to catch your kid with his wiener in hand or grinding on top of the life-size stuffed pony you bought her for Christmas. She may love that pony in a different way than what you intended, but damn it, let her be. In a literal case of different strokes for different folks, some kids start earlier than six, and according to e-mails we've received, some people don't attempt masturbating until well into their fifties. A long list of personal and anatomy-related factors go into when, why, and how often you rub one out. Maybe your parents caught you at a young age and chastised you, so now you associate orgasms with guilt and you only jerk off when you are 100 percent sure no one else is in the house. Maybe you masturbate three times as much on Thanksgiving because Turkey Day of '97 was the day you "accidentally" discovered the porn mags your dad had been hoarding under his mattress. Or maybe you never had a desire to do it because your hormones were never raging. We're all unique snowflakes, guys. There are a few uh-oh-don't-do-thats when it comes to masturbating, such as don't masturbate in public. That's not cute, and you're creeping everyone out, sir (or ma'am—women can be creepy too #feminism). Of course if a child does this, he or she just needs to have a heart-to-heart with a parent about when and where is appropriate for personal pleasure. Not the case with adults. If you've ever lived in New York City, I'm sure you've seen a drunk guy (or four) with his hand down his pants as he stares at you in a crowded subway car while you try really, really, really hard to just focus on Candy Crush until the next stop. In the future, you can take a photo of that person for evidence and then call the cops because that shit is not only creepy but illegal!

Regardless of your masturbatory past, the one thing we can say for certain is that learning to make yourself cum will do wonders for your sexual future. If you understand how your own body works, you can take that knowledge into partnered sex and give constructive feed-back that will benefit the both of you and probably make you a more relaxed and happy human, because dopamine! Whenever a listener sends us an e-mail about not getting what they want and not knowing how to give their sexual partner instruction, our response is almost always "So you know everything you just said to us? Say that exact thing to them!" You can also use masturbation as a nonthreatening way to educate your partner—"I touch myself like this" is much sexier than "You suck at this."

In fact, while masturbation is often thought of as a solo activity, its partnered version is underrated. I highly recommend you try out mutual masturbation. It's as easy as it sounds. You just sit next to each other . . . and then you masturbate. I do this with Stephen, and I wish I had thought to suggest it earlier on in my sexual career. It turns me on so much to see him jerk off. Honestly, it's better than porn, and I looooove porn. There's something about watching the guy you love grabbing life by the (his) dick and going to town. And he's making all these sexy noises and it's just . . . Damn. Be right back.

Mutual masturbation is also a fun activity if you're not ready to have sex, either in general or with that particular person. It's a wonderful way to get to know someone's body and how they move and how they like to be touched. Plus, no risk of STIs or pregnancy. Hooray!

When Masturbation Gets . . . Sticky

When I was younger, I thought my boyfriends should only masturbate while thinking of me; otherwise it would be cheating. If you think the same way, I totally understand, but I promise you're wrong. I vividly remember being on my high school boyfriend's computer and looking at his browser history while he was in the bathroom. Tears welled up in my eyes and lightning shot through my veins as I came across a Google image search of "Lindsay Lohan boobs." I. Was. Livid. He came back from the bathroom expecting us to go to the diner, but nope. Not on my eighteen-year-old insecure watch! The poor guy. I yelled at him and asked him why he would do such a thing. He should have told me that I was being ridiculous, but bless his heart, he just stumbled over his words for a minute or two until I dramatically stormed out of his house. I came right back inside once I realized that he was my ride home. We begrudgingly talked it out, and over time, I realized that expecting your boyfriend to think of only you when he masturbates is unrealistic, controlling, and insecure. He and I dated for several years after that fight, and by the end of our relationship, we were watching porn together, and it was the best sex I ever had with him. What a turn that took! I sometimes wonder if my anger over him looking at other women on the Internet was due to my constant need to be in control or if it was from my childhood. When I was five or six, I started to notice that my dad's office door was locked a lot of the time, and it gave me this sinking feeling in my gut. That feeling ultimately led me to sneaking onto his computer and seeing porn at *way* too young of an age. I recall feeling furious at him. *This* is what he's looking at?! Those ladies looked like they were crying in pain, and he was just sitting there looking at it instead of helping them!?! When you're a child—specifically when you're *me* as a child—sex noises are often interpreted as cries for help, and I was a very helpful, sweet kid who couldn't stand the sight of adults crying. So, yeah, a few issues under the surface there.

I have "caught" Stephen masturbating and shamed him for it one or two times. Okay, three times. Again, even though I know it's silly, I still have a twitch about it. I honestly would not care if, say, I went to bed earlier than him and he came to bed wanting to fuck, saw me asleep, and just jerked off while I was sleeping. For some reason catching him doing it while we're both awake gets me fired up. It's always during a phase when we're not having that much sex and I'm feeling a smidge guilty about it. We both work from home, so we're *always* around each other. In my logical brain, it makes total sense that he'd jerk off in another room, especially if he comes on to me and I hit him back with "Eh, not now. I'm tired/I'm busy/my stomach hurts/wah-wah-wah/periods." However, if I'm home and I sense that he's downstairs masturbating (it's my sixth sense), part of my brain is all like *"Not on my watch, mother-fucker!"* I wish I could tell you why I still have that reaction as an adult woman, no matter how rarely it happens, but the important part is that I recognize it's a dramatic and unfair reaction to have. One huge reason why: I do it too. When I'm stressed out, I don't really want to have sex because it's hard for me to be present, but I usually want to have an orgasm to help relieve stress and I want it the fastest, easiest way possible. For me, that requires a vibrator. The only time I can understand being upset over your partner masturbating is if he or she is constantly turning you down for sex and then the second you're apart, they're jizzing all over the couch. That hurts. But it requires a conversation, because there's a reason your partner doesn't want to fuck you, and you deserve to know what that reason is, whether it's understandable or not.

Krystyna

Butt Stuff

Everyone has a butthole. It's kinda comforting if you really think about it. But not every person wants their butthole to be licked or touched or penetrated. This anal disinterest might be because they've never had their butthole "properly" licked, touched, or penetrated so they don't associate that part of their body with pleasure. It could also be due to fear of pain. Perhaps the only thing you've used your butthole for is to eliminate waste, which you believe is its sole purpose, so the idea of anything going *into* your anus seems just plain wrong. Totally understandable. *But!* There are powerful pleasure centers to be found in and around your butthole that are waiting to be explored, *especially* if you're a man, because men have a pot of gold inside them, and by "pot of gold" I mean the prostate. More on that shortly.

My Anal Résumé

During high school and my first two years of college, I didn't entertain the idea of anything going in or around my asshole, and I certainly never considered touching any of my partners in that area. The following is every single piece of information I had about anal sex up until college:*

---

* These are factually inaccurate.

* Gay guys do it in the butt.

* Ladies in porn sometimes do it in the butt.

* You can't get pregnant if you do it in the butt.

* Apparently Jesus won't hate you if you do it in the butt, but he'll really hate you if you do it in your vagina.

* A lot of girls *hate* getting it up the butt.

* A lot of guys *love* giving it up the butt.

There was a rumor that went around my high school about a girl who had anal sex with her new boyfriend while her parents were at work. She would have gotten away with it except for the part where she shit all over the carpet afterward and couldn't get the stains out. I never personally verified this rumor, but I remember a three-day stretch when it was all anyone talked about. Life is so simple when you don't have to pay bills or go to work. That rumor was the first time I had ever talked to my girlfriends about anal sex, and we were all on the same page about it: Fuck. No. I forget everyone's reasoning, but mine was a fear of pain and the fact that it didn't seem logical for something to go *inside* the butthole. I also think I villainized most high school boys for wanting anal. Maybe some of them didn't deserve that, but I knew too many stories from friends about guys pressuring their girlfriends for anal sex and then making the girl feel like a prude for saying no. That's some bullshit right there. But what those stories also did was make me think that girls who like, or tolerate, anal sex were considerably more desirable to boys than those who abstained.

With my first boyfriend, there was zero talk about butt stuff and, much to my relief, zero attempts at it. I was with my second boyfriend during high school and some of college, and we attempted anal sex a few times, but I was always in too much pain and stopped him before he could get his penis in there.

Fast-forward two years and I'm in New York City, finishing up college and living in an apartment with a few friends. I was single and had a crush on about five dudes from either school or work or interning, and occasionally I met someone at a bar who wasn't a complete douchebag. These were my golden sex years, which I'll always look back on with such fondness. It was when drinking alcohol was exciting and going out to clubs felt a little rebellious. Whenever my girlfriends and I would go out for a night on the town, I'd always get this exhilarating rush and think, *Wonder who I'll be going home with later!* Then, while dancing to some Lil Wayne and pouring a third glass of whiskey down my throat, I'd hit up a minimum of two of my current crushes. The rush of who it was gonna be that night was thrilling. Chasing dick made me feel so alive!

One rainy night out, I texted Nico, a crush I knew from a previous job. We had had sex a handful of times before this night, and it was always A++. I really, *really* liked Nico and would have loved to take our fuck-buddy status into monogamous territory, which was likely the reason I ended up doing what I did at his apartment later that evening.

I got to his place and we chatted. At this point, we were both stone-cold sober. I was probably trying to impress him with whatever cool shit I could think of off the top of my head. The chemistry between us was and will probably always be electric. While we were talking, all I kept thinking was *I hope we have sex, oh my god, can we please just have sex, we should have sex right now, why are we even talking?* Then I realized that I had my period. How I forgot that fact is beyond me. I love having sex on my period when it's with a boyfriend. But it had never been something I had the desire to do with a guy

I was casually sleeping with. When I realized I was on my period, I got pissed. Nico asked me what was wrong, and when I told him, he replied, "That's okay. We don't have to do anything!" Oh, but we did, Nico. We fucking did.

I mean, I wasn't bleeding from *every* orifice. I made Nico sit on his couch with his pants down, I blew him for a little bit, and then *boom*. No lube. No mind-altering substances flowing through my veins. Just anal. I sat down on his dick with my back facing him and, after a few deep breaths and light teasing, proceeded to bounce on his penis as it went in and out of my butt. I was *so* impressed with myself. My first experience having actual anal, sans alcohol. *That's* how much I liked that dude. He had no idea that it was my first time doing anal until about four years later when Corinne and I interviewed him on the podcast, and I wish I could have captured the shock and awe on his face when I told him. It was satisfying to see him as impressed with me as I was with myself in that moment. We high-fived. I rule. It should be noted that this is *not* the approach I recommend for anal play. We'll get to that in a minute.

Stephen and I successfully had anal sex twice during the first three years of our relationship. It felt much better this time around because he was an expert at foreplay and appreciated the Art of the Butthole Tease. The third and, up to this day, final time we had anal sex was when I was bleeding an alarming amount afterward and took my bloody ass on over to the emergency room. That last experience left a bad taste in my mouth and an even worse feeling in my butt. It made me realize that I don't like anal enough to risk tearing my asshole apart. However, I've taken a few workshops that dove into anal and have had numerous discussions about it with Stephen, my guy friends, my girl friends, guests of the podcast, sex experts, and listeners who have e-mailed us. Here, dear readers, is what I've learned.

Things to Consider for Straight Men Who Wanna Put Their Dick in a Lady's Butthole

Be Good at Everything Else First

* If you've not yet mastered fingering or fucking or going down on a vagina and making a woman cum clitorally, there is no way in hell you can be good at anal. I promise.

Put Something Up Your Own Ass

* You need to know what it feels like. Plain and simple. It'll give you an entirely different perspective and approach when thinking about going up someone else's ass. My suggestion is to use your own finger or, even better, have your partner stick *her* finger up there.

* If you're a dude who has already felt the sensation of something entering your ass, awesome! You can skip this part.

* If you're a dude who will never, under any circumstances, allow any object or person near your ass, *grow up and get over yourself. You're never gonna know how to fuck a butt if you've never at* least *had a pinky up your own.*

* If you're a dude who thinks it's "gay" to have something up your ass, spoiler alert: it's not gay. You're just being narrow-minded and ignorant. Every man has the equivalent of a G-spot in their asshole, and if you're going to be so stubborn about anal penetration, you're missing out on having a P-spot orgasm (did I mention we'll talk more on that later?).

Get on the Same Page

* Have a conversation about it. Conversations can improve your *sexual compatibility*. It can be as simple as saying "What are your feelings

toward anal sex?" Maybe she loves it, maybe she's never done it, maybe she's hesitant. Understand where she's at with the subject, and you can both move forward from there. Also, talking about sex with the person you have sex with can be really hot and act as foreplay.

Tiny Ass Baby Steps, Yo!

* Foreplay is *key*. Never start anal off by simply sticking your dick in her butt. I'm sure most of you know that already, but if you didn't, you're welcome. Important: you don't treat a girl's butt the way you treat her vagina. Every woman's anatomy is unique, but I recommend starting by slowly stimulating her clit. She needs to be turned on before you move south. Use your tongue, use your hands, use a toy. Whatever you use, start out slow and soft, and maybe even after a few orgasms work your way from her clit to her anus. Then use your tongue/hands/toys in that area.

* Anal beads and small butt plugs are both excellent toys to use as prep, after some light touching and licking. For butt plugs, I recommend starting out with the smallest size first. Lube it up, slowly stick it in, and it will lightly stretch you out.

Lube, Lube, Lube

* Anal + Lube = ♡

  My favorite lube is the one Babeland sells. It's water-based, tasteless, and odorless, and it leaves your skin feeling smooth. If you don't live in a major city with a retail store, you can order it online and have it shipped (www.babeland.com).

* Anal − Lube = ☹

  Putting things up your butt without any sort of wetness, whether that be lube or spit, just turns into a round of bumper cars at the carnival.

Check In with Each Other

* Make sure your partner is enjoying what's happening or, at the very least, not in pain. Sometimes the main thought going through one's head during ass play is *Huh . . . This is new.* Which is neither good nor bad, but you need to make sure everyone is cool with what's happening. You can do this and still be sexy about it. "Does this feel good?" "Do you want it harder?" You don't have to take an improv class at UCB to be good at this. You just need to be *present*.

Have a Sense of Humor If Things Go Awry

* Shit happens. It might get on your dick. It might get on the bed. I mean, what did you expect? You're putting something inside the hole made for poop to come out. Just don't shame the person. The last thing anyone should do to their sexual partner is make them feel bad over something they can't control. If you're not mature enough to handle a little shit on your dick, you're not mature enough to be trying out anal.

* Have towels nearby just in case. You can never be too prepared!

Now let's talk about doing butt stuff to guys, because this is a world that my eyes have recently been opened up to, and it's just so fucking fun and unbelievably arousing for the both of you. Ladies and gentlemen, allow me to introduce you to the P-spot. Aka the prostate. Aka the male G-spot. Aka the game changer.

Male P-Spot Orgasms

Everyone with a penis has a walnut-size gland located in the middle of their pelvis, in between their penis and rectum. It's a reproductive organ that secretes prostate fluid, which is part of what makes up semen. When a guy ejaculates, the prostate helps drive the fluid out through the urethra and onto a lady's face or a hand or a guy's butt or a girl's butt or whatever it is dudes cum on and in.

About a year ago, Stephen came to me with his phone opened up to a porn site. I was hoping that meant we were going to watch porn together and not touch each other for twenty minutes and then go at it really hard, but what he showed me was so much better. It was a demonstration video, and the ingredients included one bed, one man, zero clothes, and an Aneros Helix Syn. Aneros is a company that manufactures prostate stimulators, and the Helix Syn is the specific model the very naked man uses in this sexy video. First, he's lying down on a table, dick up. He starts jerking himself off using a ton of lube and eventually makes his way down to playing with his ass. Then he lubes up the Aneros, slowly sticks it inside his rectum, and continues to jerk off. There's one point in the video when he stops touching himself and gently starts to thrust his pelvis up and down. Ugh, this is *such* a hot video to watch, you guys. Once he's thrusting for a minute or so, you see his penis—still rock-hard—start to pulsate. Then, after maybe five-ish more minutes, still with his hands out to his sides, he begins to convulse and ejaculate. It was the craziest orgasm I've ever seen. I had no clue a guy could cum in more than one way, especially not like *that*. Stephen wanted to buy one, and I was 1,000 percent on board.

When the Aneros arrived at our doorstep, Stephen decided he wanted to explore it solo in order to get a full handle on it. He later tried to describe what this new, earth-shaking type of orgasm felt like, and my eyes grew wide in wonderment. When we first used it together, we fooled around a little, then I sat back and watched him insert it as he jerked off. Holy. Shit. When he came, his entire body was convulsing, and it lasted *way* longer than his non-Aneros orgasms. I'm going to let Stephen describe how it feels, as I'm sure it's much more helpful to get a man's perspective on this one:

It feels like you're having two different orgasms at the same time, like the Aneros orgasm happens in tandem with your normal orgasm. While you're cumming, and for a little while afterward, you feel your asshole pulsating uncontrollably.

—Stephen

It's not just the sensation. The amount of fluid that comes out of him is a much larger amount than usual. I've always heard guys talk about how hot it is to see a woman having an orgasm and I kinda sorta got it, but after seeing Stephen cum with the Aneros in, I totally get it. I'm a believer. I've seen the light. If you're interested in exploring the wonderful world of prostate orgasms and curious to see what it looks like, type in "Aneros orgasm" on Google and you'll see a bunch of options. There are also blogs about it, and the Aneros website has a lot of information and frequently asked questions (www.aneros.com). My personal favorite FAQ is "Does this mean I'm gay?" Uh, *no*! Men who are born straight don't just put a finger up their butthole one day and all of a sudden turn gay. That's not how it works. Also, a lot of my gay male friends strongly dislike having toys or fingers or penises in their butts (they stick to mutual masturbation and blow jobs), so enough with the gay assumptions.

Anilingus, aka a Rim Job, aka Licking a Person's Butthole

The last thing I want to cover in this brilliant and eye-opening section about butt stuff is some good ol' ass-to-mouth action. I've heard this act referred to as "eating someone's ass out," but that to me sounds repulsive and makes me think I'm going to contract the bubonic plague. Anilingus acts as a great opener to the aforementioned activities, especially since foreplay is such an important element to butt stuff. Your anus has a large amount of concentrated nerve endings, making it a sensitive area. So sometimes kissing can be just as stimulating as a big ol' dildo up the bum. If you're curious about specific techniques, my personal move is to start out with slow kissing and work my way up to rapidly making out with the person's ass. That doesn't sound so hot when I type it out, but I promise it's a good time.

I never entertained the idea of licking someone's ass until a few years into dating Stephen. One night, in the middle of foreplay, I went to give him a blow job when a light bulb went off and I thought, *Hey, hows about you lick his ass?* And so I spread his legs, ventured on down, and did just that. Stephen is into it and I enjoy doing it, just not every time we have sex, so I file that move under Things I Do on Occasion.

Like anything involving buttholes, you want to take precautions, such as

* make sure your partner wants this done to them, or make sure your partner is okay with doing this to *you;* and

* always shower beforehand, for your own safety but also out of respect for the person licking your butthole.

This is a fun time for people of any gender or sexual orientation. Of course if you don't want to do it, don't! If the idea of licking a butt or getting something put up your butt sounds weird to you, that's probably because it *is*. Sex in general is weird, and every person has their own comfort level, which is constantly changing and evolving with time and experience. These are all optional activities you should explore (or not explore) at a pace that feels good to you. Some people go their entire lives without ever having something in or near their butthole, while others get pounded in the ass on the regular, and both are completely acceptable life paths. You do you.

Krystyna

Three-Ways

Ever since I downloaded a three-way app on my phone and talked about my first experience with Stephen and another woman on the podcast, the questions have been rolling in about everything from how to propose a threesome to your significant other to what kinds of rules you should set prior to the clothes coming off. Here is my official guide to three-ways. Godspeed.

To give you some background, I had one threesome prior to being with Stephen. It was with two male models from a reality show called *Hot and Handy,* in which male models make over your apartment and, no, I'm not kidding. I was one of the lucky gals who had her living room made over by seven devastatingly handsome men. When I met them, my jaw dropped, and I immediately understood why a lot of guys say dumb shit to hot women. Their faces gave me diarrhea of the mouth. Within an hour of them being in my home, I blabbered on about my love for the original Broadway soundtrack of *Spamalot* and how my parents' dog pissed all over my mom's good rug and she's so mad and, oh boy, she really loved that rug, ahhh, do you guys want a beer? Me neither, who drinks at 10 A.M ?! I certainly don't, LOL.

I learned a few things from that experience, the first being that male models aren't good at painting walls red. You *always* use two coats with a dark color—come on, guys. A week after we filmed our episode, I started casually seeing and sleeping with one of the models.

Let's call him Alex. I wanted to reward myself and fuck a guy purely based on the fact that he was visually stunning. (Girls can be scumbags, FYI.) About a month into sleeping together, another model from the show—we'll call him Danny—met up with us at "da club" for drinks. He was the best looking of the hot bunch but would tell me stories I wish I could un-hear. My inner douchebag wanted to put a finger over those beautiful soft lips and tell him to stop talking, but I didn't because I'm a good person and also because I wanted to make out with him later.

After a few hours of dancing and drinking, we all went back to Alex's SoHo loft apartment for another round. I truly had no idea anything sexual was going to happen between the three of us. We hung out in the living room, had a drink, and played one of my favorite childhood games, Trouble. Then I decided I was pooped and went to Alex's bed, leaving the Hottie McPerfectFaces to hang out and continue chatting. I closed the door, took off my dress and bra, and sank into the bed. Not even ten minutes later, Danny came in and lay to my right. Then, in a very exciting turn of events, Alex came in and lay on my left. Ohhhhh shit. It's. Going. Down. There was no discussion. It just flowed naturally, as if they'd done this before. Let me tell you, having two sets of well-manicured man hands all over your body is just . . . it's a real treat. I can barely recall the sex—not because I was drunk but because I kept repeating in my head *OMGTHISIS-HAPPENINGOMGTHISISHAPPENING.* It lasted for twenty glorious minutes. No one came, but at least one girl had a great time and immediately texted her roommates about it while lying next to them. (Me! It was me!)

The three-ways following that one couldn't have been more different. I had been dating Stephen for over four years and had recently fessed up to a cuckolding fetish, meaning I fantasize about my partner having sex with someone else in front of me. The term was originally used to refer to men, and because I'm a woman who has the fetish, the technical term is "cuckquean," but that just sounds like the literary equivalent of making women's razors pink, so I stick with "cuckold." You may be wondering where the fuck this strange desire came from, and I'm not sure, nor do I care. Dissecting a kink is like having to explain why a joke is funny. You've spoiled it.

So Stephen, upon hearing the news that I was interested in having him fuck another girl while I'm chilling in the bed next to him, was so upset and confused and didn't know what to think . . .

LOL—just kidding. He was *immediately* on board. We talked it out for a few days and decided to download an app, formerly called Thrinder. It's like Tinder but for three-ways. We went with an app because the idea of hitting on a random girl at a bar didn't seem feasible to me. How the hell are you supposed to know if she wants to have sex with your boyfriend while you're lying there next to them? Thankfully there was an app for that, and I soon experienced the monster that lives inside us all when we start to swipe across another human being's face and go *"Ew!"* because their nose is sort of crooked or the left side of their hair is kind of weird or they don't have a job because they're too busy standing in front of the bathroom mirror making a duck face. After days of talking to several women through the app, we finally decided to meet up with one, whom for the sake of this story and me not getting sued we'll call Lisa.

The first thing Stephen and I needed to figure out beforehand was how fast or slow we were comfortable moving. Would we try to fuck her on the first date? Is it even a date? Does she just come over to our apartment? Or do we go to hers? Do people fuck the first night or nah? Can I just sit in the corner with my vibrator while they do all the work or do I have to go down on her? Before we could land on answers to any of these questions, the conversation took a sharp turn into us having really hot sex, incorporating all these scenarios into our dirty talk.

As I discovered purely by accident, this is an excellent way to toy with the idea of a three-way if you're curious but unsure but maybe you'll like it but maybe you'll storm out in a jealous rage. I followed my heart and my vagina, and they were both telling me to stop talking about it and start taking action.

I made Stephen do most of the communication over the app since the entire point of my fantasy was for him to be into this girl. We met up downtown for a drink with the understanding that this was purely to talk and get to know her. Having the weight of "Are we gonna fuck?" on my shoulders the entire night would have ruined the vibe for me. I can't be my charming and wonderful self if the possibility of having sex later is lingering in the back of my anxious girl brain. I operate best when I know what to expect.

On the night of the date, Stephen and I each spent hours over-thinking our outfits and hair and shoes. It was equal parts strange and adorable because we were nervously excited to take a girl out on a date. Luckily we both need to get to know someone before we sleep with them, so we were already starting out on the same page.

I remember twiddling my thumbs like an idiot while we waited outside a coffee shop for her to show up. We kept thinking every girl walking down the street was Lisa, and I eventually turned to Stephen and said, "We gotta chill, otherwise this chick is gonna smell our nervousness." I'd never felt like such a dude before! Having gone on dates only with men, I'd never gotten nervous because I felt like I had the one up.

Lisa finally showed up and we got coffee, which led to martinis, which led to a few glasses of whiskey on the rocks, which led to us standing outside the bar at midnight, taking out our calendars so we could compare schedules and get this three-way on the books. I've always dreamt of a career so consuming that I had to plan my three-ways weeks in advance.

Now, if you're new to the three-way thing or if you are like Corinne, you probably want to skip the talking and get on with the fucking. Stephen and I are talkers. We'll talk to each other all day and all night. I'm always amazed that we haven't run out of things to talk about. Talking is important to us and necessary in order for us to feel comfortable enough to be intimate with a person. But what the fuck do you even say? And how up front should you be? Should you flirt more and question less? It's weird because all three of us knew this was purely a sexual situation with no possibility of going beyond that, which was a first for me. Here are some questions/topics I remember asking Lisa about:

* I want to explore cuckolding and am really into the idea of you and Stephen fucking each other. Is that something you'd be into?

* Have you ever been with a couple?

* Have you ever done this before?

* When was the last time you got tested?

* What turns you on?

* What are you like in bed?

* Are you straight/bi/lesbian/other?

* Would you want to come over to our place?

Like I said, we're talkers. Fast-forward to a few weeks later, to Stephen and I frantically cleaning every crevice of our apartment. I'm a neat freak and always make a point to have the place nice whenever people come over. Stephen? Not so much. But I'll be damned, that motherfucker swept the floors, including behind the couch. He made the bed. He cleaned out the refrigerator. Oh, it didn't stop there. He purchased brand new sheets for our bed. He got a deluxe mattress cover. He went to Fairway and purchased enough groceries to feed a family of seven. He was basically June Cleaver, if June Cleaver's only motivation to maintain a nice household was pussy. He even traveled to a hardware store in Brooklyn to buy extra two-by-fours to reinforce our shitty IKEA bed. Why? What did he think was going to happen? That he would tear apart our bed with his dick like Thor? After the third time he asked me about his hair, I had to chime in with a pep talk about the art of being chill.

The plan for the evening was to have Lisa come to our very clean apartment and drop her stuff off, we'd all go get a few drinks at a nearby bar, then we'd come back to our very clean apartment. The conversation over drinks felt more like nervous foreplay, but I was liking the vibe we had going on. If I'm being truly honest, I mainly just wanted to rip the Band-Aid off and get it over with. I wanted to have this first experience with Stephen under my belt because I knew it would ease the nerves and allow me to enjoy future three-ways more.

We had drinks and talked for almost three hours, way longer than we planned. We all walked back to the very clean apartment and plopped on the couch. I was still nervous at that point, so I broke out my green tin of weed, and Lisa and I smoked a little. Then she and Stephen kept talking about shit I wasn't interested in, like the cultural significance of *Dune* or Joseph Campbell's influence on George Lucas, so I just butted in and said, "Hey, so are we gonna fuck or what?" Not the most romantic line, but it got a laugh and that's all I ever care about.

We headed to the bedroom and the clothes came off. So far, so good. Then Lisa proceeded to give Stephen a blow job. This was unlike any other blow-job technique I had ever seen. It was a ninja blow job. Her tiny little hands went all over the place, but she had the right rhythm and apparently Stephen liked it. A lot. I got jealous, but I didn't show it. I just sat with it for a second. It wasn't a strong enough feeling to speak up. I didn't want them to stop. I was just feeling a little incompetent about my BJ skills, which I've never felt before and didn't expect. There was no intercourse between Lisa and Stephen, even though we were all comfortable with the idea, probably because they both have dominant sexual personalities. I knew this because we'd talked about it over drinks. What I didn't know was that they'd end up basically wrestling each other, both with the mindset of "No, I'm gonna fuck *you!*" Despite their mismatch, it was still hot to watch, and my vibrator and I really enjoyed each other.

There's this thing with me and orgasms, though. Once I cum, I'm done. My brain immediately switches to something completely unrelated to sex. So I'm lying there, post-orgasm. They're still semi-wrestling and hooking up, and I'm thinking, *I have to get up and go pee. Do I do it? Should I just go? Do I say something? Should I interrupt?* I hemmed and hawed as they wrestled and wrestled, and I decided it was best to just get up and go. I really don't think they noticed, but Stephen claims he did. It was weird that I left without saying anything, but oh well. You live and you learn. When I hopped back into bed, they were just lying there hanging out, and we chatted, smoked a cigarette, and I remembered that Stephen had a shitload of food in the fridge, so we made snacks. Another lesson learned for future threesomes: no sleeping over. That got weird. Stephen was in the middle and it seemed like he was overly cuddly with me to make sure I was feeling okay about everything, and then at one point he turned his back and put his arm around her, and I was like *Nope! Not today, sir! Time to get up!!!*

Lisa was still asleep, so Stephen and I went out into the living room. I feel shitty being honest about this part, but I really, really, really wanted her to leave. I felt like I ripped the Band-Aid off, it was mostly fun, a little uncomfortable at times and somewhat nerve-racking, but I did it and I was happy it happened. She finally awoke and could tell I wanted her out. Again, shitty of me. I wasn't sure why every fiber of my being wanted her to leave, but once we said our goodbyes and she shut the door behind her, I turned to Stephen and the words just came out of me: *"Does she suck your dick better than me?!?!?!??!?!"*

That was a fun conversation that tested our comfort and honesty levels as a couple. But my favorite part about our first three-way was that I felt even closer to Stephen after that. I somehow loved him *more* after seeing a girl named Lisa give him a ninja blow job and wrestle him. Love is weird, you guys.

One of the most common questions I get from couples considering a three-way is "But what if I get jealous!?" It is completely normal and okay to get jealous—even if you're the one who set up the three-way because you're the one who fantasizes about it in your spare time.

That said, if your relationship isn't 100 percent solid, do not attempt a three-way. I repeat: do not attempt a three-way. That's like having a baby to fix your marriage. Or throwing a lit match into a pile of hay that's doused in gasoline. Or eating an entire Thanksgiving meal and then going for a run. Not a good idea.

Also, if you're in a relationship that's solid but the idea of incorporating a third person turns you off, don't have a three-way. Not everyone should have three-ways. They're not something you do to impress your partner. They're something you do when the idea of it turns you and your partner on and you've both talked about it and are on the same page. And, yes, even if a three-way does turn you on, you still might get jealous. And then you woman up, take mental note of what Lisa was doing with her hands, steal a few of her ninja moves, and diversify your portfolio of blow-job skills. It's a win-win.

CORINNE

Period Sex

You think period sex is gross? Not more gross than the notion that so many women are walking around during the most stressful week of the month not getting fucked. There's no medical issue with having sex while on your period. So why is it an assumption that when I'm bleeding it's blow job week? First off, that's insensitive. On top of unused baby real estate dripping into my underwear, you expect me to get on my knees with low iron levels to suck on your perfectly fine D? *No bueno.*

For some reason men think they are doing women a solid when they "allow us" to fuck them on our period, but *au contraire, mon frère*! This just in: having sex with a chick on her period is like getting a flash pass to an orgasm—we will cum so hard and so easily that you might actually think you've found the elusive G-spot!

Plus, no matter what your actual day job is, you can play doctor when your female partner has her period, by making your dick a literal healing wand come to life. You heard me right. A 2013 study published in *Cephalagia* concluded that boning while menstruating helps relieve the migraine headaches often associated with that time of the month.* So for those readers with penises: go ahead, with her

---

* A. Hambach et al., "The Impact of Sexual Activity on Idiopathic Headaches: An Observational Study," *Cephalagia* 33, no. 6 (2013): 384–89, https://www.ncbi.nlm .nih.gov/pubmed/23430983.

consent, let your dick enter her vagina's bloody hallways, and proudly proclaim *"The doctor is in!"* You can tell her Corinne and Krystyna said that was okay.

Now on to logistics. We've all seen the nasty stain that horse head left on the sheets in *The Godfather*, but guess what? The saying "put a towel down" doesn't just exist because it's comical; it exists because that's what you need to do. Blood is a very easy stain to get out if treated quickly with soap and cold water. I don't know this because I'm a murderer. I know this because I have been happily having period sex for years. All I'm saying is, like, hey, do you really go to the gym enough to make that eighty dollars a month worth it without taking a towel for the road every now and again? Gym towels are the perfect size for dangling around your neck while you work out or putting under your or your partner's ass as you thrust your way to pleasure town (believe me, the phrase "pleasure town" is more disgusting than any period sex I've ever had).

And, women, while day one or two might feel like ass with that signature period diarrhea, after the initial terror that a period can be has passed, I suggest sex. But *please, please, please* remember that a period does not make you invincible. You can still get pregnant during your period (although it's unlikely) *and* you actually have a slightly higher risk of getting an STI because your cervix is a little bit more open during menstruation so there's more room for, um, "shit to get in." Man, why aren't I a doctor by this point?*

---

* Amanda MacMillan, "6 Things You Should Know About Having Sex During Your Period," Health.com, February 9, 2015, http://news.health.com/2015/02/09/6-things-you-should-know-about-having-sex-during-your-period/; Amy Kraft, "Is It Safe to Have Sex During Your Period?," EverydayHealth.com, last modified February 17, 2016, http://www.everydayhealth.com/news/it-safe-have-sex-during-your-period/; and Hanna-Brooks-Olsen, "6 Very Real Concerns About Period Sex & How to Deal," XOJane.com, August 27, 2013, http://www.xojane.com/sex/6-very-real-concerns-about-period-sex-how-to-deal.

CORINNE

Sending Nudes

Sending nude photos can be a fun part of foreplay. Unless, that is, they're unsolicited dick pics. Here's a little tip to all the penis havers out there: Stop. Sending. Your. Dick. Pics. To. Women. You. Don't. Know. Yes, there are women out there who might get off on a rando penis in her inbox. But is this a gamble you want to take? Because if she is not one of those women, your odds of having a sexual relationship of any kind with her are low. A photo of a penis we want to see is glorious. A photo of a penis we don't want to see is weird and annoying. Rule one, in comedy and in dick pics: know your audience.

Regardless of your stance on taking and sending nude photos, one thing is clear. We need to stop making this a life destroyer. Don't discount someone's worth because a photo of their pussy is in a folder on your desktop. A very unfortunate reaction to the endless number of celebrity nude photo leaks is to think he or she shouldn't have taken them if they didn't want them seen by the world. No, no, no, no, a million times no. Just because you're an asshole and expose someone's private photos doesn't mean that person deserves it. You're just a huge piece of shit with poor morals and a lot of self-esteem issues. Nude photos are a form of sexual expression, and everyone has a right to privacy of that expression if they so choose. Unfortunately, not every state sees this as a legal issue. In fact, before 2013, only three U.S. states expressly prohibited nonconsensual disclosure of sexually explicit images and videos. Thankfully, now more than thirty states and the District of Columbia have laws against it, according to CNN legal analyst Danny Cevallos.*

Despite the danger, sending nude photos is one of my favorite pastimes. If and when you decide to do so as well, here are five rules I highly suggest you follow:

1. **If you're under eighteen, just don't do it.** As tempting as it can be, having nude photos of yourself floating around while you're still under the rule of your parents is a bad idea. In fact, it's dangerous for both you and the recipient because *technically* you're distributing child pornography, and that'll be tough to explain at future job interviews.

2. **A butt. A boob. A beaver. Keep it to one *b* at a time.** Think of sending nudes as technology's answer to burlesque. A burlesque dancer never takes her whole outfit off at once; she does it one glove at a time, and magically that makes her an *artist* instead of a sex worker. Additionally, if anyone tries to screw you over in the future by distributing your nudes, at least they'll be avant-garde as fuck.

3. **Keep your face out of it.** Until you're in a very committed relationship in your twenties or thirties, your face just needn't be a part of the equation. While many men will ask to cum on your face during your lifetime, very few will cum to the thought of your face. So skim the fat.

4. **Be selective.** A nice body is like a new relationship—you want to share photos of it with the world, but . . . don't. As naughty

---

* Danny Cevallos, "Revenge Porn: How to Make It Stop," *Opinions* (blog), CNN, March 9, 2017, www.cnn.com/2017/03/09/opinions/revenge-porn-legal-action-needed -cevallos/index.html.

and fun as it is, sending nudes really loses its oomph when everyone has a copy. Your nudes should be limited edition, collector's item, Disney vault shit. Only the biggest fans get them and then they're deleted forever.

5. **Before you click SEND, have a quick meeting with your friend Reality.** The truth is, any nude photo you send can be "used against you." So before you release it into the void forever, fully understand that many people beyond the intended recipient could see this; it could end up anywhere on the Internet; depending on your occupation, it could get you in trouble; someone could try to use it to blackmail you in the future; and, worst of all, it could be met with a lukewarm response. Every nude photo I've sent was something I deemed okay for public consumption. Do I *want* my nudes to go viral? Nah. But do I wake up every day knowing that's a possibility? Absolutely.

Krystyna

That's a Thing?! (Yep)

So we've talked through masturbation, anal, threesomes, period sex, and sending nudes. But that is just scratching the surface. Here are some sexual moves, acts, and fetishes you might not even know exist:

* **Crush Fetish.** This fetish entails getting aroused by watching a person crush objects, food, bugs, or small animals with his or her feet. It's more popular than you might imagine. The federal government actually passed a law specifically criminalizing interstate sales of so-called "hard crush" videos, which depict the squashing of vertebrate animals like rabbits and puppies.

* **Hierophilia.** This is a sexual attraction to religious or sacred objects, like crucifixes or ministerial garb. However, it does not count when your mom sees a yarmulke on a cute dentist's head at shul.

* **Anthropophagolagnia.** This lovely condition involves fantasizing about raping and then cannibalizing a person. There is nothing funny about this paraphilia except that it has its own Facebook group with 52 Likes. No Patrick Bateman to be found, sadly.

* **Rusty Trombone.** Eating out a guy's asshole from behind while jerking him off. This seems relatively harmless but also only for the very long armed and talented.

* **Wobbly H.** A three-way with two men and one woman in which one man is having sex with the woman from behind while she's sucking the other guy's penis. The H refers to the shape created by the participants. It's no coincidence that "hell" is the first word that comes to mind upon imagining myself trying not to bite a guy's dick off while getting railed, doggy style, by the other guy.

* **Blumpkin.** Giving a guy a blow job while he's defecating. Off the top of my head, I can think of about 13,673 good places and times to suck a guy's dick. "On a toilet" and "While he's taking a shit" are *nowhere to be found on that list.* But I'm not here to judge, so to any blumpkin-ers, I salute you (and spray a big ol' hit of Febreze your way).

Rape Fantasies Are a Thing but Should Probably Be Renamed

Krystyna

This goes without saying, but no one *wants* to be sexually assaulted. Never. Ever. No one. That doesn't mean that some people don't fantasize about a scenario in which they can play pretend and act out seemingly "forced" sex in a safe, consensual environment. If this confuses you, think back to when you were a kid and would play make-believe with toy guns or lightsabers or swords. Just because you hit your friend's arm with your plastic sword doesn't mean you wanted to cut their hand off. You were just playing pretend and having fun getting lost in the imaginary world you'd created. Now just trade swords for sex.

At the beginning of my relationship with Stephen, we were lying in bed together one night and an arousing light bulb went off in my head. I turned to him with a smile and said, "Hey! So tomorrow, if you wake up before me, I think it'd be so hot if you started touching me gently, while I'm asleep, and worked your way up to slowly fucking me." We kept talking about it a little more and he was on board. Score! The next morning he did exactly what we had talked about, and holy shit was it hot. I had never done that with another person before, but his openness intrigued me and inspired me to explore more of what I want. We did this for about the first year of our relationship, and I noticed that the more we did this, the longer I would pretend to be asleep throughout the entire thing, which made it even hotter to me. Pretending to be taken advantage of became the most exciting element, and, ironically, the deeper into playing out this type of scenario we got, the more bonded I felt with Stephen. I'm sure there's some smart-person psychologist theory as to why this is, but when it comes to sex, breaking everything down into a science ruins it for me. The only way I can put it without turning myself off is that this fantasy opposes what I want in my everyday life, allowing me to experience the ultimate form of control. As a woman, I've had men say some vile shit to me on the sidewalk, at the office, in school, and at work. In all of those instances, I hated those men. They made me feel out of control, as if my body wasn't my own. As if it was theirs to comment on and gawk over. I've had a few strange men even touch my ass in public, and I felt the fire of a thousand suns take over, making me want to fucking murder them. The rage stems from someone taking away my control over my own body. Playing pretend and telling Stephen that I want him to take control over my body feels empowering because it is my decision to do that, and most importantly, I ultimately have all the control. If he does something I don't like, we immediately stop what's happening and regroup. While I don't think this needs to be stated, you never know, so I'm going to state it: *I don't actually want to be raped.* I have no interest in any kind of one-sided forced sex, and it makes me sick when I think about the people on this planet who think they can use the bodies of others as their living playthings. Now that that's out of the way, *I absolutely want to be consensually raped by my partner.* The good news is, *that's not rape!* A rape fantasy is adult make-believe. It's the kinky grown-up's version of "playing house"—and it's not making light of anyone's sexual assault.

To me, this fantasy is more about playing with the boundaries of control, and the only circumstance in which I could feel comfortable doing that is in the presence of a sexual partner I love and trust. Some people don't need to love the other person to act this kink out. That's totally fine, but I personally need to have a loving connection in order to feel that comfortable letting go. After learning about how often rape happens, how it turns someone's life on its head, and how stigmatized victims of sexual assault are, it's hard for me to put the word "fantasy" or any other positive word after "rape." Even though the names of several kinks don't translate literally into the acts associated with those names, I've heard too many atrocious stories and have spoken with too many men and women in tears about their own rape to have that word included in something I enjoy. If you prefer, feel free to replace the term "rape fantasy" with "ravish fantasy." It's the only term I've heard as a replacement for "rape fantasy" that doesn't make my eyes roll. And if you need more reassurance and pointers in this arena, Corinne's got you covered.

CORINNE

Having Your Cake and Fucking It Too

A FEMINIST PERSPECTIVE ON RAPE-ISH RENDEZVOUS

In his *Psychology Today* blog article on the subject, Michael Castleman, M.A., explains that the notion that women who have rape fantasies subconsciously really want to be raped was debunked decades ago. Modern psychologists usually attribute the fantasy to one of three things:

1. **Sexual Blame Avoidance.** This means that many women feel guilt or shame because of their desires, but a desire in which they are forced alleviates them of responsibility. Ah, well, if this doesn't describe being a woman in a nutshell . . .

2. **Sexual Desirability.** Like the plot of a supermarket romance paperback, it's kind of hot to think a dangerous, wild man may be so enthralled with us that he has to enter us, whether we like it or not.

3. **Sexual Openness.** People who are sexually explorative and have accepted this about themselves often feel free to try

out scenarios in the bedroom that they would never want to experience in real life. (This last one is me. It annoys me that anything mildly kinky, such as a rape fantasy, always has to be linked to some weird shit going on in my brain. Can't a gal just want to be pretend forcibly fucked? Let a bitch live.)*

One-third of women admit they occasionally daydream about being forced into sex, so if you're one of them, cancel your therapy session because everything's gonna be fine, fine, fine. And if you or your partner is into this, whether it's simply getting a little rough or acting out a taboo scenario, this is where the open, honest conversation part of control play comes in. Regardless of who brings it up first, you need to make sure both or all parties involved are on board and understand each person's physical boundaries. Do you want to get hit? If so, how hard and where on your body do you like it? How do you see this playing out? Do you want to plan a day when you're lying on the couch and your partner comes home from work and starts touching you? Without talking it through, control play is not impossible, but not having a dialogue about it beforehand takes away the whole "play" part, which is the entire fucking point.

---

* Michael Castleman, "Why Do Women Have Rape Fantasies?," *All About Sex* (blog), *Psychology Today* online, August 1, 2015, https://www.psychologytoday.com /blog/all-about-sex/201508/why-do-women-have-rape-fantasies.

CORINNE

There's a Law for That

In the era of Trump, it seems like the laws that govern us as sexual creatures are becoming more and more stifling each day. That said, there are plenty of sex laws that have been around for years that prove that legislation in this department has always been strange, and mostly ridiculous:

* In Anniston, Alabama, if a woman loses a game of pool, it's illegal for her to settle her bet with sex. This seems (a) unfair and (b) based on a previous incident.

* In Harrisburg, Pennsylvania, it's illegal to have sex with a truck driver in a tollbooth. Specific, but safety first.

* In Oxford, Ohio, it's illegal for a woman to strip while standing in front of a man's picture. Ohio hates waste.

* In Connorsville, Wisconsin, it's against the law for a man to shoot off a gun when his female partner has an orgasm. In theater, we call that "chewing the scenery."

* In Tremonton, Utah, no woman is allowed to have sex with a man while riding in an ambulance. In addition to normal charges, the *woman's* name will be published in the local newspaper. "After

getting quotes from a PR firm, Joy started fingering herself with her left hand and dialing 911 with her right."

* In all of Arizona, you can't have more than two dildos in your household. After all, it's called a California closet, not an Arizona closet.

* In California, it's illegal to sell stuffed items resembling breasts ("boobie pillows") within a thousand feet of a highway. Finally a legal system that fully understands that breasts are public nuisances.

* In Indiana, it's illegal for a man to be sexually aroused in public. Indiana or bust (in the privacy of your own fucking home, you perv).

the only one who knows

I AM A WOMAN HEAR ME ROAR.. also quietly sob of desperation

I only have sex with grandpas, please help

High School Sweetheart wants my booty?

Sexless in marriage. Th

Atheist Vegan Female in an Interracial Relationship

Holy Shit I'm Single

Is it fucked up that I'm not fucked up?? A perspective you might not have heard before?

STAYED WITH A GUY JUST FOR HIS DICK??

Sexles

LLS [feeling confident in ar difference relationship]

My exgf telling my parents I'm suicidal after we break up

My Best Friends Boyfriend threw a pur at me and sprained my wrist....but I'm bad guy???Should I tell her parents?

Juicy Booty Office Romance

en relationships are complicated G OUT IN HIVES. Help.

HECK I THINK I'VE ACCIDENTALLY MADE AMATEUR PORN

Fiancé used dirty talk to cheat

BF's sister sending nudes to him?????

Feeling like an emotional rollercoaster with spouse's infidelity. Help!

Helping My Best Friend on His Girlfriend???

My girlfriend considers porn cheating

I'm The Crazy Girlfriend You Always Talk About

My BF was physically abused by his ex GF?!??

IN A 2 YEAR AFFAIR AND CANT LET GO :(

disgusted d

oyfriend and I want but don't know y to go about it

Is it the D or is it love? I slept with my ex's best friend and now I can't stop thinking about him.

Getting divorced, thanks to you bitches

ENGAGED....A AND DIVORCE PROCESS

Wait, now I'm Bipolar? Well fuck me gently with a chainsaw.

Brother sleeping with his twins wife

eating still cheating? woman?!

Girlfriend left me for being transphobic???!!!

I want to be a slut so I can get my girlfriend back... long story, need advice

am elf

How to be a good respectful ex-girlfriend

Should I prostitute myself to my husband?

can't fuck the guy I like - help!

I WANNA ABANDON MY HUSBAND AND RUN AWAY TO NYC BUT ONLY WHEN IM HIGH BUT WHEN IM HIGH THAT'S MY HAPPIEST HELPPPPP

Help! I accidentally came out as bi over a podcast and now my mom hates me!

ARE WHITE MEN SUBMISSIVE OR IS IT JUST ME?

He says I'm beautiful, they say I'm ugly, I just want to be understood

ht cheat on my ar god help me

My husband regularly forced himself on me, and now I am having an affair with a married man

I Slept With One of My Girl-Friends and I Have a Boyfriend – Now I Feel Like a Chea

Is he really sexually harassing me in fro the kids?

Don't be Polyamorous Without Asking Your Wife if That's Cool First

MY EX HUSBAND HAS A BABY WITH HIS FIANCÉ AND I AM SAD.

found my gay porn too ht us closer together

Hetero-man with painted nails *question

Threesome with my ex BF | bad idea or not??

SUGAR DADDY CHEATED

Stranded and (potentially)

cam girls cheating?!

my dad is cheating on my mom and im the only one who knows

My husband cheated & it didn't ruin our marriage.

AM I CRAZY OR IS MY BOYFRIEND AN ASSH

So my wife found my gay porn too and it brought us closer together

PLEASE Help! I cheated!

Masturbation is wrong; phone snooping is a-ok

his ain't right.

How do you tell the tinder guy who ended things that you are pregnant?!

threw up in your bed, but you didn't have to give me Chlamydia

Holy Shit I

OLD BALLS [feeling confident in a 10 year difference relationship]

My 17 yr old son's girlfriend is threatening suicide if he leaves her

He's married and I cheated

Do you think it's ever ok to marry young?

ted...

Should I get married? No really

My Wife is using a dating app to secretly flirt with other women

He Lied about Using Protection & Used the Pregnancy to Control Me

I fucking snooped

How to propose to a man

g like an emotional spouse's infidelity. He

g My Best Friend Girlfriend???

RELATIONSHIPS

I cheated...

regnant and disgusted y my husband

My ex-boyfriend is now my ex-girlfriend, and I cannot thank you enough for our friendship.

Dumped that cheating piece of shit...but now what??

Help! My boyfriend and I want to fuck a girl but don't know the right way to go about it

So it turns out my wife is gay...

My ex is asking me for help after getting a girl pregnant. Wtf?!

onal cheating still cheating? e other woman?!

I read my boyfriends diary because I'm a dick

my bf wants to put his dick in everyone's pussy (consensual - not like trump)

eated and i am d with myself

I cheated on my wife with her sister

My husband's girlfriend

I'm a slut with a husband

to have sex friends

Why couldn't he have cheated on me and fucked me? I wouldn't have minded.

I have been cheated on by every single partner, what's wrong with me??

I'm drunk and my wife won't have sex with me

Sometimes cheating happens... and it really helped!

My girlfriend cheated on me, and it made me so... Horny???

Urgent! I might cheat on my husband. Dear god help me

35, heartbroken and had a lesbian affair with my next-door neighbour. What do I do next?

Do I leave the man of my dreams to chase DICK?

my husband got propositioned during a lap dance to have a threesome....

Is my husband a human piece or garbage, or am I batshit crazy?

My best friend can't stop boning her married boss

He's emotionally abusive

Why doesn't my husband want some wife approved pussies!??

CORINNE

Keepin' It Cas'(ual)

Casual sex—yes, it's the fast food of sex. Feels kinda dirty, but that doesn't mean every once in a while it doesn't hit the spot juuuuust right.

I'm great at casual sex because I have the magical power of being able to compartmentalize my feelings—super useful during casual sex, super hurtful to a lot of people I've been in relationships with. It's a treat that seems to be enjoyed openly by men and secretly by women—not because we don't like it, but because we are concerned about our reputations. I'm a self-titled "slut" (*yawn*—who cares?), and people have the misconception that because, when I'm single, I enjoy not only casual sex but a lot of it, I have no standards. This is simply not true. Almost every time a gentleman I've slept with but haven't spoken to in a while shows up for his *Guys We Fucked* interview, I find my hand patting my own back. I'm selective AF. It just seems I know what I want and I know how to get it.

While perusing the Internet for resources that might help me tap into slut culture beyond my own experiences, I came across a *New York Times* article from 2005 describing a bunch of women who had gotten together to discuss *The Hookup Handbook: A Single Girl's Guide to Living It Up.** After recuperating from discovering this is a text in exis-

---

* Alex Williams, "Casual Relationships, Yes. Casual Sex, Not Really," Fashion & Style, *New York Times,* April 3, 2005, http://www.nytimes.com/2005/04/03/fashion /casual-relationships-yes-casual-sex-not-really.html?_r=0.

tence (and after scouring my bookshelf to make sure I had not already purchased it in a *Sex and the City*–induced blackout), I quickly noticed the concerns of women having casual sex then were identical to the concerns popping up in our e-mail inbox a dozen years later. It wasn't the risk of STIs or the chance of accidentally falling for these men that plagued these women. It was the fact that it would "raise their number"—the total number of men they'd had sex with in their lives. We have somehow convinced ourselves that quantity is actually more important than quality and that more is not better. We eagerly settle for one mediocre partner for a while instead of sleeping with a bunch of men who pique our interest in one way or another for a few weeks at a time. While many screen-printed tees argue fries are better than guys, fries and guys certainly have very little in common. In-taking fries raises numbers that matter, like cholesterol and blood pressure, whereas in-taking guys merely raises a number that you should never even be asked to divulge in the first place. But if you still find yourself feeling bad about this digit, do what I do: remind yourself that Gene Simmons from KISS has slept with over 4,800 women and his band isn't even very good (flinches).

Krystyna

One-Night Stands

WHEN IT'S GOOD, IT'S GREAT—
WHEN IT'S BAD, IT'S FUNNY

Ah, one-night stands. The ultimate gamble for everyone. We all should have a sense of humor about one-night stands, especially because a lot of them go awry and it's not the end of the world. Maybe he got whiskey dick. Maybe her cat kept coming into the room and clawed your balls. Maybe the entire apartment smelled like feet and you didn't notice it until the next morning. Maybe the person didn't tell you they lived with their parents and you found out after walking to the bathroom naked and running into a very angry dad in the hallway. That shit is hilarious! Maybe not in the moment, but it will be, a few years down the road. A one-night stand isn't something a person should feel shame over. However, it might be something you end up regretting, and that's perfectly okay. You can feel like shit about a one-night stand, but don't let it end there. Feel like shit, figure out why you feel like shit, reflect, and decide if you have valid reasons to feel like shit, then identify what you want to do differently next time so you can avoid feeling bad. And for the love of all that is sexual, *use protection.*

I've never had a one-night stand because I rarely have orgasms from intercourse alone, so I didn't see the point. If I was blessed with a vagina that orgasmed from just a penis, I would have had one or two or twenty-seven one-night stands by now. I came very close to having one once. It was with a British man I met when I was twenty. He was five years older, and, yes, his accent made my vagina tingle. We danced and talked for hours, and he dropped that he was not only staying at the Waldorf Astoria but also in the Presidential Suite. About 80 percent of me knew this was utter bullshit, but the other 20 percent was like "Maybe he's telling the truth. Let's go see what a fancy hotel room looks like!!" So we walked on over to the hotel and into his private elevator. When we reached his floor, the doors opened and my jaw dropped. I had no way of knowing if it was technically the Presidential Suite, but god damn, it was fancy. We headed over to his bed and started taking off each other's clothes while sloppily making out. The second his underwear came off, I looked down and said to myself, *"Nope!"* And then I said out loud, *"Nope!"* He had the biggest penis of anyone I had ever seen. It was like two cans of soda stacked on top of each other. I was horrified and failed at hiding it. That wasn't gonna fit in there. Hell no. His penis was so big that I didn't want to stay in the same bed with it. I needed to leave immediately. He was bummed out, which I totally understand. I'm not sure if he felt the same as a guy who gets a similar reaction for his dick being too small, but I could tell he was frustrated and that this happens to him a lot. While I never want to make a person feel bad, especially when they're naked and vulnerable and their gigantic monster dick is throbbing in my face, the beauty of it being a sorta kinda one-night stand was that I didn't feel the need to sit there and console him or even continue to talk to him. I got dressed, wished him well, and peaced the fuck out!

One-Night Stand Calling Cards

Sometimes it's hard to say goodbye. To a dying relative, to a friend who lives across the country, and definitely to the dude lying next to you Sunday morning whose name you think is Jonathan, but it also could be Justin, John, Andrew, or Oscar. Men's names are pretty bland. Should you find yourself in a stranger's bedroom, here are some notes you can leave on their pillow after a one-night stand:

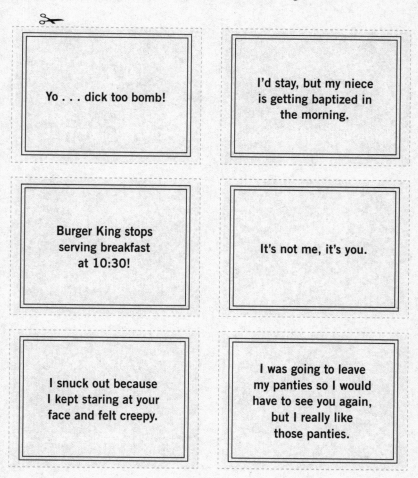

Yo . . . dick too bomb!

I'd stay, but my niece is getting baptized in the morning.

Burger King stops serving breakfast at 10:30!

It's not me, it's you.

I snuck out because I kept staring at your face and felt creepy.

I was going to leave my panties so I would have to see you again, but I really like those panties.

YOU'VE BEEN F*CKED

YOU'VE BEEN F*CKED

YOU'VE BEEN F*CKED

YOU'VE BEEN F*CKED

YOU'VE BEEN F*CKED

YOU'VE BEEN F*CKED

The Importance of Communication

Krystyna

Wanting a partner to be 100 percent sexually compatible with you right from the get-go is a nearly impossible expectation and a lot of stress to put on an early relationship. That said, the more comfortable you are with your sexual partner, the better the sex is, the more open you'll be to trying new things, and the more satisfied you both will be. The good news is, if you sense a disconnect between you, there's a cure for that. It's called communication. I'm not talking about the vaguest college degree hundreds of thousands of dollars can buy. I'm talking *talking*. Say what's on your mind. What are you so afraid of? Your feelings and concerns are there for a reason, and you need to talk it out to uncover why. Maybe your fuck bud really is being inconsiderate *or* maybe you're projecting your feelings from a previous relationship. Either way, getting to the bottom of this shit should be a priority. Yeah, it can be scary. But we're all a bunch of pussies when it comes to being vulnerable—before we find out that honest communication makes a relationship better. And if it doesn't? You part ways and move on with your life. Better to know now than ten years, two kids, and one mortgage down the road.

So it all comes down to talking. Simple, right? Well, apparently it's not always easier said than done. You might shoot the shit with your close friends about blow jobs and hand jobs and rim jobs, but do you talk about it with the person you're actually having sex with? According to the majority of e-mails we receive, you do not. Communication leads to better, more satisfying relationships, whether it's with a fuck buddy, boyfriend, wife, sugar momma, etc. People don't always know how to approach certain subjects with their partners, so here are some sample questions that have helped me out in my relationships.

WHAT DO YOU FANTASIZE ABOUT WHEN YOU MASTURBATE?

It's good to be up front about your kinks, quirks, and fantasies. This isn't a subtle question, but subtly is for politicians, not your pussy. You might not get an honest answer, depending on how comfortable the other person is, but you'll get great insight into what turns them on. And who knows? Maybe you'll discover you share the same "fucked up" fetish. Or maybe he/she has a kink that you've always been curious about. If I was single, this would be one of the first questions out of my mouth, because the conversation that comes from it is basically verbal foreplay. Speaking of fetishes . . .

DO YOU HAVE ANY KINKS?

You can ask this question only if you promise not to judge the other person. And if you think you'll get judgey, ask yourself why that is. Did you have crazy religious parents who made sex out to be the work of the devil? Sorry about that, but your parents don't know shit about shit if that's their logic. I've talked to people about the seemingly strangest stuff, like how much they love rolling themselves up in a rug and having women step on them in high heels, or how they get *so* turned on by the crunching sound of someone stepping on bugs (I swear on my life this is true). Nothing fazes me these days. Once you start asking this question, just know that you might encounter a few kinks you didn't know were possible. Whatever you do, don't make a face as if you just saw your childhood dog get run over. That's rude. Just because you don't like something doesn't mean everyone has to also not like it. One person's "classic go-to" is another person's "only on our anniversary" and someone else's "only if the world is burning."

HOW DO YOU LIKE TO CUM?

This question is especially important to ask women, since pussies be mad varied! Do you use a vibrator? Are you one of God's chosen ones who can cum vaginally? You don't have to get more specific than that if you don't want to. I always forget that people aren't as open about this shit as I am. I like to dig deep with questions, like: How often do you masturbate? Where's the weirdest place you've ever put your dick? Has your dick ever been out of commission for a few days because you jerked off too hard? Do you have a testy vagina that is sensitive to certain fabrics? Do you use sex toys, and if so, which ones?

WHEN WAS THE LAST TIME YOU GOT TESTED?

If asking this question feels weird to you, just know that being pro-active about your sexual health is one of the best things you can do for yourself and your partners. Knowledge is power. This also shows a level of responsibility that eliminates any room for judgment toward your sexual past. You shouldn't be judged on this regardless. However, if you're a person who has a lot of sex *and* you're on top of your game by being responsible and prioritizing your sexual health, that's fucking sexy.

HOW ELSE DO YOU PRACTICE SAFE SEX?

I can't stress this enough: when you have sex with a new partner, *use protection*! If you're a guy who can't get hard with a condom on, there are things you can do to counter that, like wearing a condom every time you masturbate. Eventually, you won't give a fuck what's on your penis, you just want to cum. This will retrain your brain to the sensation of a condom. It's important to note that a guy might not want to fuck you that much if it means altering his daily routine. And that's okay! On to the next.

If you're a man who sleeps with women and you're paranoid about pregnancy, even if you use condoms, be up-front and ask your partner if she's on birth control. Just be aware that she might be one of many women whose hormone levels go haywire on the pill. (I am one of those women and it is not fun.) If that's the case, respect her decision to not want to be a raging psychopath.

Even if the person you're fucking just got tested, some sexually transmitted infections take weeks or months to show up in a person's blood or urine, and it's possible that the person never shows any physical symptoms. Some STIs can't be tested in men, such as HPV (human papillomavirus). First of all, that is some Bull. Shit. Secondly, that means if you're a woman who sleeps with men, you could contract HPV without the dude ever knowing he gave it to you, which could end up with you getting genital warts or, worse, cancer. I'm not trying to scare you into not fucking, but it's important to know this shit. HPV is extremely common, and there are forty different types that we know of. Most types of HPV will go away by themselves and do not cause cancer, but if you're a cigarette smoker or if you have a disease that makes it difficult for your body to fight off infections, you are at a much higher risk.* Ladies, make sure to get a Pap smear every three years in addition to STI tests before a new sexual partner. If you add condoms on top of that equation, you're being pretty fucking safe!

---

* "Learn: Human Papillomavirus (HPV)," Planned Parenthood, https://www.plannedparenthood.org/learn/stds-hiv-safer-sex/hpv.

DO YOU WANT KIDS?

This question is important if you're headed toward being exclusive. It doesn't matter if you want kids or not. The important part is that you're both on the same page with it. I asked Stephen this question right before we became monogamous. Having a baby one day (in the far-off future) is something I want in life, and I wanted to make sure he could see himself having a kid or two before I took the relationship any further.

CORINNE

You [Don't] Complete Me

Through our podcast, we have come to realize that most of the relationship problems people have stem from their poor sense of self-worth. If there's one thing we want to drive home, it's that *you are in charge of you*. And you need to be in working order before you can expect a relationship to succeed.

Before you can find, or at least fully enjoy, another person's love, you must believe in yourself. If you are in a relationship already, it's essential that the person believe in you. While Panera and I did not work in many ways, he was the first boyfriend to see in me what I saw in myself, and while I know I would've been successful with or without him, he certainly expedited the process. Of course it's most important to be your own biggest cheerleader, but every now and again even the strongest amongst us needs a break where we get to float on someone else's admiration of us.

If the person you are with doesn't believe in you—or, on the flip side, if you don't believe in them—it's just not going to work. Schedules can be altered, relatives can be ignored, cunnilingus can be coached, but believing in someone comes from deep down in the pit of your stomach. It cannot be concocted or fabricated or learned. And without belief in your partner or a partner who believes in you, you will suffocate your purpose, that person's purpose, or, most likely, each other. No matter how stupid a passion seems, remember that anything someone feels passionately about cannot be stupid because it's the reason they get up in the morning. Unless their passion is crafting stuff they sell on Etsy. Then run for the fucking hills.

Thoughts on Monogamy

Krystyna

OR ONE PENIS FOR THE REST OF YOUR LIFE, MWUAH HA, HA, HA!!

Like the majority of you, I was taught that romantic relationships are monogamous. No one took me aside and explained this concept, but all the examples of romantic relationships in my life consisted of two people who were seemingly faithful to each other. Most of my friends lived in a two-parent household. Every movie I watched as a child that featured romance centered around one boy and one girl who had eyes only for each other. There were no Disney princesses going around trying to get some dick on the side. It was clear to me from a young age that entering a relationship meant shutting down all possibility of giving or getting attention from anyone except your partner, which always seemed so finite and a tad suffocating, even before I had a full grasp of the idea of partnership and the rush of emotions that comes with falling for someone.

I think most people go into their relationships with the expectation of monogamy, which makes total sense. Especially when that person makes your heart thump out of your chest and all you want to do is sit on the couch and stare into their eyes all day. But for me, even at an early age, monogamy felt like a lot of pressure to put on any one person. I thought, *Okay, if I meet someone and fall in love and we stay together and eventually get married, that means I can be with only that one person until the day I die, unless we want to go through the emotional and financial pain of getting a divorce.* It almost made me scared to fall in love because that meant I was trapped forever and had to jump through a hell of a lot of hoops to get out.

That feeling has been present during every single adult relationship I've had, yet I never brought it up because it felt taboo to question a concept that's been around for centuries. When I met Stephen, our first conversation was way more honest and candid than any I'd had up until that point. I was shocked that he went into such personal detail about sex and dating, and with such ease! As if he'd been talking that openly his entire life. It was refreshing to hear another person be that forthright. When we started dating, I sheepishly brought up my feelings on monogamy and how it didn't make sense, even though I had thoroughly enjoyed all my monogamous relationships. I fumbled so hard trying to put it into words because I didn't want to scare him off. "I mean, it's not like I want eight boyfriends or anything, but it's a lot of pressure—kinda like you're in a prison but the prison is pretty great but, like, there's only one other person in the prison and it's just you and them forever until you die and you can't get out but there are all these windows so you *see* everything on the outside—" Without missing a beat, he said, "Yeah, that's because it's not natural to be attracted to *just* one person for the rest of your life." My jaw dropped. Just hearing him say that and understand what I meant was fucking mind-blowing, and, ironically, it made me want to marry the shit out of him!

Stephen and I are not in an open relationship in which we can sleep with other people in our spare time, but establishing the mutual understanding that it's okay to be *attracted* to another person felt so freeing, and the types of conversations we have about people we're attracted to are conversations I never thought possible. I used to think that if your boyfriend talked about another girl being attractive, that meant he was a scumbag. I mean, if all your boyfriend talks about is how hot other women are, then, yeah, fuck that noise. But for me, the small act of being able to verbalize my attraction to other guys, and being totally okay with him doing the same, lifts all the pressure I had placed on relationships.

Monogamy is not for everyone, but it *is* for most. On the flip side, polyamory takes a certain kind of person and shouldn't be something you're coerced into. In the same way people feel pressure to be monogamous, don't feel like you should want an open relationship if you truly don't. You gotta follow your heart *and* your genitals, and decide what it is you want out of a relationship. I've cheated one time in my life, and it made me feel like a garbage person. I told my then boyfriend the next day, and he was heartbroken. Hurting someone you love, who gave you their heart and trusted you with it, is a feeling I hope I never have to experience again. Some people can cheat and not feel broken afterward, and good for them, but that sure as shit ain't the case with me. I've been cheated on twice. Once when I was sixteen and again when I was twenty-two. Immediately following each infidelity, I spiraled into a dark, depressing mental state, feeling as if I'd lost all control over who I was. The second instance led to a six-month bout of bulimia, my desperate attempt to feel in control. Looking back, I realize that each infidelity happened because my boyfriend and I both went into the relationship assuming it was monogamous and avoided talking about feelings that would force us to challenge that idea, which is why an attraction to another person felt so shameful.

People cheat for all sorts of reasons, and it doesn't automatically mean they are dissatisfied in their current relationship. I've said it before and I'll say it again: chasing dick makes the world go 'round. Meeting a guy I'm attracted to, pursuing, and finally getting to have sex with him fills me with this electricity and excitement that one only gets whilst chasing dick. The thrill of the chase and that subtle emotional dance leading up to sex makes me feel like a fuckin' *woman*—a ravenously sexual and divinely powerful woman. To desire and be desired is a beautiful feeling, you guys.

That said, just because you have an itch doesn't mean it *has* to be scratched. Maybe just a light tap will do the trick, or maybe you leave it alone. We don't get every single need met in a relationship; human beings are too complicated for two people to have the exact same set of desires. Stephen and I have taken the conversation from "Other people are hot too!" to "What are your thoughts on sleeping with other people?" and it turns out that we aren't on the same page with that. After discussing where our comfort levels are, I learned that he would not be okay with me sleeping with another person without him there. A three-way? Totally cool. Whatever we do sexually, he strongly prefers that we do it together, in the same space. When he told me this, I wasn't disappointed, because my love for him is much stronger than wanting to hit the town and chase some dick. Our relationship is so fucking important to me. I wake up every day and thank Beyoncé (Jesus isn't my thing) that I met Stephen. Maybe his feelings on monogamy will change a few years down the road, but maybe they won't and that's okay.

CORINNE

Relationshipping

While most people would categorize a romantic relationship as one of life's must-haves, if relationships came in cup sizes at Cold Stone, I would order Like It, not Gotta Have It. In 2016, I wrote an article for *Glamour* magazine about being newly in a relationship (with James) after spending four years in New York City as a single woman. The reactions to the update of my Facebook status made me want to grab all my friends by the shoulders and shake them vigorously.

"You deserve it!"

"Congrats!!"

"OMG—I knew it would happen!"

"Huge—it's brutal out there!"

These weren't messages of support for a woman who had just come home from war, kicked meth, or gotten her Ph.D. These were because I got a fucking boyfriend. As butterflies-in-my-stomach as I felt to have met James, these idiotic comments from the people in my life gassed those butterflies to death immediately. Had they not been watching all the other stuff going on in my life for the past four years? Did they not see me co-create a podcast that topped the iTunes comedy charts, sell out the world-famous Comedy Store, have my television debut, get signed by the biggest talent agency in the world . . . and give a fucking *TED Talk*?? I felt like Mugatu in *Zoolander* because it seemed to me that everyone was, indeed, taking crazy pills. Every day I had spent in the United States as a single woman seemed to have been, unbeknownst to me, another quick step down the Oregon Trail. Will today be the day Corinne dies alone in a ditch with no one to cover funeral expenses costlier than a shallow dirt grave?

As a culture, we have somehow come to the conclusion that the ultimate goal for everyone is to find "the one." *Bam.* Pass Go, collect $200. You. Are. Done. But I think there are many people out there who actually function better solo and are afraid to try it out because we have somehow deemed being alone "giving up." By promoting this notion of "the one," we have bred generations of people who think there is something peculiar about them if they can't find the aforementioned one . . . when maybe the one was you all along. As long as we keep straight, single women questioning their value, men will always be the hottest commodity . . . and they just *aren't*.

As a single woman, I had become what I had always wanted to grow up to be: a better version of me. In all honesty, I was succeeding so much in my life that when I met James I was kind of annoyed. Why did the cosmos send me someone so wonderful in the middle of my career hot streak? Also, where had Cupid been all those weekends I was eating Domino's Philly Cheese Steak pizza and Netflix-ing *Californication* because masturbation isn't really my thing? Yes, James and I immediately had a connection that was undeniable, but did dating him mean breaking up with myself?

It didn't and it hasn't, and, honestly, if a die-hard Hillary Clinton woman and a Trump-or-bust man can make it through the 2016 presidential election, I'm pretty confident in our staying power. We challenge each other, support each other, and cause trouble on the Internet like no other couple I know. We also live down the block from one another and have never even thrown a "Hey, why don't we move in together?" to see how it lands. We are very separate people who come together several times a week because we are each other's favorites.

Being single isn't better or worse than being in a relationship. It's just different. I love James and am grateful that someone came into my life who is dry witted, unapologetically himself, and able to recognize that the fast food chain with the best Diet Coke is definitely McDonald's, but every now and then I reflect on that time I went to see *Spring Breakers* alone on a Friday night. It was great—both my elbows had armrests that night.

This brings me to another type of relationship, the kind of relationship people recommend when they can't quite seem to make a monogamous one work: the open type. Do I believe that a couple can truly be okay with sharing each other sexually? I do. Do I believe the main motivation for this is wanting their partner to experience other pleasures? LOL. That's some Grade A horse manure if ever I've heard it. I believe some couples have realized in order to fuck other people while in a relationship it's only fair they be okay with their partner fucking other people too. It's a brush with reality, not martyrdom. And the whole concept of open relationships would be way less annoying if we just acknowledged this as a sexually progressive society. I don't care how Zen or in touch with your sexuality you are. No one's dying to have their partner fuck someone else (unless they derive sexual pleasure from that, in which case it's still selfishly motivated, and that's okay). It's Bargaining 101. *To get what I want, I must be okay with my partner getting what they want.*

My main qualm with the new popularity—or, really, reemergence in popularity (from olden-times)—of polyamory, open relationships, and multiple partners is this notion that not only can we have it all but we *should* have it all. When did we decide we deserve everything? In my experience, I always get much stronger results when I go without. The best change comes when I have that hunger. Is being with only one person a challenge? Yes, but it's that fight that keeps it alive. *I am going to fight to make this work.*

I've dirty-talked with married men in open relationships, and as much as I didn't want this to be so, they just feel to me like pussy gluttons. So hippie-ish in their sex that it made me not want to fuck them. One guy in particular, whom I had a crush on for years, I had no interest in fucking anymore, because why did he deserve that? Why did he deserve me? He gets to fuck me and then go home to his wife and fuck her too? It almost seems like people were cheating so much they just found a way to make cheating okay. To say "You know what? This is too hard." A relationship has a high value because it *is* so fucking hard. Instead of working on our commitments, we have worked out ways not to fully commit.

We have become weak, and I think it's because we don't go without anymore. Do I think monogamy is natural? No. But I do think it's the stronger choice. Week after week I sit behind the *Guys We Fucked* mics and try to be as understanding about every sexual situation as a human being could possibly be asked to be. I've wrapped my head around not being born with the genitalia of the gender your heart is, not being able to be romantically attracted to anyone, wanting to get your balls stepped on, and feeding someone to an unhealthy weight because their fat jiggling makes your dick hard. I think you should be able to pay to have sex and choose to be paid to give sex. I get watching your boyfriend have his dick sucked by another woman. Choking, spanking, cutting. Even the notion that your brain is telling you to fuck a kid (as long as you *never, ever* act on that). But what I have not been able to wrap my brain around is telling the person you love more than anything in this world, "Sure, go out and snuggle with someone else. Hold someone else's hand. Laugh at someone else's jokes." I've considered all this stuff, even reasoned with myself that maybe I'm old-fashioned or insecure. Not the case. I'm the same person I've always been: Someone who has worked really fucking hard for everything she has. Someone who walks into her apartment every day and is so thankful that she kept at her dream of comedy even when it meant losing friends, relationships, and money, and spending a good portion of her twenties miserable, poor, and in a tiny bedroom infested with mice. The point is, I went without and that's why I appreciate this all so much. My face lights up when I walk out onto my terrace because I know what I did to get that terrace. And, mostly, because I know what I did without.

Passover has always been my favorite Jewish holiday because it's the only one I can think of that truly builds character. You've never had a slice of bread that tastes as delicious as the slice of bread you have after Passover. Over the course of those eight days I would feel almost dead. But at sunset on that eighth day I never felt more alive.

I used to be into the concept of an open relationship. Hell, I was in one. But I was okay with it because, at the time, I thought it was the best I could do. I didn't love him enough to fight for him, and I knew he didn't love me enough to go without additional sex. But before that? Before that I was dating Panera. And I loved Panera so much the thought of fucking someone else literally made me sick. And now the thought of James looking at someone else the way he looks at me when we have sex makes me want to cut a bitch. I don't own James by any means, but I have gifted myself to him. He owns me because I gave myself to him, not because he took me. This goes for you too: no one can take you, but you can give yourself to someone.

If you're so quick to decide you deserve it all, maybe you've been too easy on yourself this whole time. You're worthy of the best things and treatment, but so is the person you're with, and maybe you can only give that to each other if it's just you two. I'm secure enough to tell my partner I'm the only one he can be with if he chooses me, knowing that I am, in fact, enough.

Krystyna

Romance and Farting

Everybody farts. Oprah, the elderly, mall Santas, Taylor Swift. You probably just farted right now, and if you didn't, you will soon. Personally, I think farts are one of the funniest things on the planet. I will always laugh at the sound of a fart. Always. Even if I'm attending a funeral and someone farts during the widow's speech. I know this because I've been in that exact situation.

As a stand-up comedian, I'm constantly writing down ideas for new bits, but nothing I write will ever crack me up quite like the sound of a fart. I'm not ashamed to admit that, on occasion, when I'm alone in my apartment, I sit around and make fart sounds with my mouth and elbow, and laugh so loud you'd think I was having a seizure. A few years ago Corinne got me for my birthday a tub of Flarp!—putty that makes fart sounds when you squish it—and that container of joy has gotten me through some dark times.

You might think it's weird that I'm dedicating a section of this sex book to farts, but they play a larger role in romance than you may realize. Sure, I'm all "LOL!" when I'm by myself and no one's around to judge me, but when it comes to romantic and/or sexual relationships, especially at the beginning, I don't even acknowledge that farting is a thing my body is capable of doing. If you're a fuck buddy, never will I ever fart in front of you. I'd rather drink from your toilet.

When it comes to farting in front of a person you like, it depends on how long you've known each other and where the relationship is headed. Every couple has their own unique "fart arc" that serves as the barometer for how comfortable you both are showing your true, gross colors. I can recall the exact moment I first farted in front of Stephen. He had been letting them rip after the two-month mark, but I was going strong (with sharp shooting pains in my stomach) for about eight months. When there are so many seemingly "perfect" examples of women shoved in your face by magazines, television shows, movies, and advertisements every goddamn day, you sometimes forget that farting does not make you an unfuckable troll. Maybe if Allie and Noah had farted in that scene in *The Notebook* when they fuck on the floor in front of the fireplace, we'd all be a little more forgiving. Stephen had been wanting me to fart in front of him in order to even the playing field and feel less shitty about doing it in front of me. Other couples might not make as big of a deal about farts, but I remember saying to him early on, "Okay, I'm gonna do it! I'm gonna fart in front of you!" and I *always* chickened out and held it in until I left his apartment. I felt much more comfortable letting 'em echo through the beautiful tree-lined streets of Cobble Hill, Brooklyn, in front of all the hot young moms pushing babies in strollers. But when I finally farted in front of him, we entered a new, much more comfortable layer of our relationship.

After you're both at farting-in-front-of-each-other status, there's no telling where you go from there. Maybe you rarely do it in each other's presence. Maybe you have a competition in which you see who can fart the loudest at the most inappropriate moment. Maybe you go up to your partner on occasion and look them dead in the eyes and, in a solemn tone, whisper, "Baby, I'm so sorry," and they go, "For what??" and you go, "For this . . ." (Cue a fart so loud it could wake the neighbors.) Or maybe you're both playing a painful game of Russian roulette to see who is going to do it first.

I'm not very familiar with how other couples approach farting. It's not something I talk about with my friends or overhear in strangers' conversations. It's not talked about much in pop culture or on Twitter or in books (*'cept this one, you lucky duck!*), but I'll tell you all about the role farts have played in my current romantic relationship because I am #brave.

Shortly after Stephen and I entered the down-to-fart stage, it became a cute, comical thing we would joke about. I was relieved to feel that level of comfort *and* be just as attracted to him. Our love was so beautiful and perfect that no bodily function could ever put a dent in it. Until The Shower Fart of 2012. I'll never forget it, though much like the memory of seeing a homeless man get hit by a prison bus on 42nd and Lexington, I wish I could.

On one sunny spring day in 2012, we banged in his beautiful Brooklyn brownstone apartment before hopping into the shower to wash the stench of sex off. Stephen was soaping up his loofah as I tried to get his flimsy black comb through my Roseanne Roseannadanna hair. We were smiling at each other and joking about whateverthefuck when all of a sudden I went to inhale oxygen through my nose, as one does when one breathes. I let out a piercing screech and ran out of the shower before Stephen even realized what happened. You ever breathe in a smell that's so bad it makes you angry? Oh boy, I have!

It took a second for me to mentally recover after The Shower Fart of 2012. I eventually bounced back, but the incident *still* comes up in conversation. It was so bad that all I have to say to Stephen is "Hey, remember The Shower—" and he'll go *"Yes. Can we please put that past us?"* It's a fair request. I got his permission to write about #TSFof2012 in this book with the agreement I'll retire that memory from conversation.

One thing I will say about farts in the context of relationships is that fart-shaming is a thing. I should know because I am guilty of it . . . a *lot*. I've yelled at Stephen for farting, I've given him that confused-but-angry Robert De Niro face, I've just said "Really?!?! Really??" and that's cunty of me. It's something I'm actively trying to work on because we've had serious conversations about how bad and embarrassed my reactions make him feel, and he's absolutely right. When I fart in front of Stephen (and, boy, do I fart), he never says anything! Even when I say "Oh no, that's was a bad one. Cover your nose. I'm so sorry," he smiles and lovingly says "It's okay. You never have to feel bad about that." Dammit, writing all this down really makes me feel like a piece of shit!

If you're a person who feels ashamed over passing gas, I understand. But also, get over yourself. Farts happen. If you can go into another room because you'd rather not audibly fart in front of your boss, go for it. That's understandable. When it comes to romance, though, have a sense of humor about it. And don't shame a person for farting, like I did. That's unnecessarily cruel, and I'm gonna shut my laptop real quick and go apologize to Stephen for being a dick about it over the past few years.

Sometimes Your Sexual Partner Can Cross a Boundary During Sex

AND IT DOESN'T NECESSARILY MEAN THEY'RE A MONSTER

Krystyna

While I have never been raped, there was one instance of something that felt sorta kinda rape-y with a former boyfriend. It's uncomfortable to talk about because (1) I don't want to make him out to be an inconsiderate asshole, because he is far from that, and (2) I didn't feel bad or upset about it afterward as much as I felt confused. But it's important to talk about this kind of shit because it's a thing that can happen when you're a sexually active person in the world.

This particular boyfriend and I had a ton of vaginal sex, but never anal. He never got his penis more than a quarter of a centimeter inside my butt until this one odd, uncomfortable, awkward incident. One weekend, we went out to a bunch of parties and drank a bunch of shitty beer. After coming back to my room, we immediately disrobed, climbed up on my bed, and started to have sex. I was drunk, but I remember all of it. There was a moment when I was lying on my stomach and he was lying on top of me. That was usually the part where he'd rub his dick in between my butt cheeks. We did that move a lot, and I loved it because (1) I have a great ass and that position gave him a wonderful view, and (2) it felt good on his penis. Of course alcohol is no excuse, but I know with full certainty that it played a major role in what happened next. He got on top of me and began to thrust his penis into my anus. My heart went into my stomach and I quietly uttered, "Hey, um . . . can you not? Uhhh . . ." He wasn't hearing me so I realized I needed to speak louder. *"Don't put it in there!"* But he kept making the attempt. It wasn't until I physically pushed him off me and screamed at him that he stopped, and I could see his face get pale with horror. He realized that what he just did was rape-y, and he knew I knew it was rape-y, and he felt like shit about it for a long time after that. I think it's important to point out that this sort of thing can and does happen in relationships at varying levels of severity and every person's reaction to this rape-y/-ish situation is different. That's okay. You can be upset or totally unfazed or angry. You can truly not give a flying fuck or you can break up with a person because of it. For me, I knew he felt terrible. He never did it before or after that night. It was a dumb drunken move, and I didn't feel violated or scared. I was very angry that he ignored me in that moment, and we talked about it until we both got to a place where we felt okay. It's the piece of advice we come back to time and time again: talk honestly about the situation and everything will be okay.

Shit We Should Probably Stop Doing in Relationships

CORINNE

Snooping

It seems like everyone I know has looked, is looking, or is thinking of looking in their partner's phone, and I couldn't be more against this idea, because besides being a blatant invasion of privacy, when you go snooping you're almost always going to find something you don't like. The catch: you weren't supposed to see any of that stuff to begin with.

The fact that you want to snoop in the first place is probably rooted in insecurity, lack of trust, or a delightful cocktail of both those things, so guess what's definitely not going to help that situation? Compromising trust even more by looking for things that you can surely feel even more insecure about. With the right mindset, any kissy-face emoji can be just as bad as walking in on your partner in the middle of anal.

Couples counselor Liesel N. Aranyosi points out, "It would be a useless cause to attempt to get facts or information by snooping, because the moment you present the 'evidence' to your partner, he or she becomes aware that there was a breach of privacy and will react defensively—wouldn't you? Defensiveness is coming from a 'fight or flight' mentality and is not conducive to having a calm discussion about what you have found out in your private eye session (be it negative, neutral, positive)."*

Snooping has been going on since the beginning of time, I'm sure, but I feel like it probably used to be a lot harder. I imagine horses and/or binoculars were involved. Also, paying people off and having a nose for any smells that don't belong to you. Way back then (the '90s), those skills were probably very necessary, but as I have only had the great pleasure of being in romantic relationships during a very technological age, any snooping situation I've been a part of has been phone, social media, or computer based.

I haven't had a ton of experience with snooping because I don't tolerate it, but the three times I've rubbed elbows with it were complete shit. The first time was in the midst of an almost five-year relationship that should've really ended after two and a half years. I had been dating the same guy from basically the moment I turned eighteen. He was my first sexual partner, my first love, the first guy I peed on, and also the first guy to snoop on me. Bonus: he was rich so he had access to some real high-tech *Harriet the Spy* equipment. Because of our having an "open relationship" without enough communication or boundaries on what established aforementioned open relationship, my thenboyfriend grew extremely suspicious of me and ended up becoming Marilyn Manson–level controlling—spying on me, having his minions watch me, paying me to "assist his business," which I would later realize was just his way of keeping me out of New York City (you know, where all the men in the world are stored), and, my personal favorite,

---

* Liesel N. Aranyosi, "Why It's Counterproductive to Snoop When You're Suspicious of Your Partner," *PsychCentral*, published October 6, 2013, https://psychcentral .com/blog/archives/2013/10/06/why-its-counterproductive-to-snoop-when-youre -suspicious-of-your-partner/.

purchasing a program that would trace my keystrokes so he could learn the passwords to my e-mail and MySpace accounts. (MySpace was like Facebook, but with songs that played when you went to the person's profile—ya know, just so you could really feel what they were feeling. When this relationship finally ended, based on trust, claims of unfaithfulness, and simply outgrowing him, I chose Willie Nelson's "You Were Always on My Mind.") This relationship actually had relatively good communication, but the issue was more that because of our age difference (he was about eight years older at a time in my life when eight years made a lot of difference) our roles were not those of partners but of person learning how to be in a relationship and relationship teacher—a dynamic that can work but usually not forever, especially not for someone like myself, who demands equality. I should've bounced when I felt the urge to try some new things, but, hey, it's hard enough to break up with a boyfriend you love, never mind break up with a boyfriend who has also become your best friend.

The second demerit for snooping actually goes to me, but in my defense, it was purely by accident. Not like a "My dick slipped" accident, like a real accident. My darling angel of a boyfriend, Phoenix (super fake name), had lent me his laptop because I was having computer issues, and while looking for a document I—hand to god*—accidentally opened his porn folder. I'm not one of those chicks who can't handle her guy looking at porn. Nay, I encourage it. I have no interest in single-handedly keeping up with the sexual needs and desires of a person, and I would not expect anyone to do the same for me. Porn, strip clubs, thinking of your ex and never fucking telling me—whatever it takes for you to not resent me for not sucking ya dry on a school night. So the problem was not the fact that the porn was there. The problem was in what kind of porn it was. It was female

---

* Victoria Beckham.

muscle porn. Like, bodybuilders. Babes who looked like they could terminate. This freaked me the fuck out because, well, not only did I not have a six-pack, at that time in my life I couldn't even do an unassisted push-up. So, yeah, I was pro-my-boyfriend-looking-at-porn if it was mostly porn of other flat-chested pale brunettes. Unfair? Kind of. But it's hard to feel confident in the bedroom after you discover that all your boyfriend seems to be jacking off to are horny gladiators.

My most recent and (fingers crossed) last experience with relationship snooping was the worst, probably because it was based on falsities. Panera had gotten it into his head that I was canoodling on the downlow with an indie singer-songwriter who frequented an open mic I ran downtown with my friend Jonesy. Joke was on him, because Jonesy was actually the person I was secretly masturbating to. Panera went through my phone one night while I was in the bathroom and found some pretty harmless flirty texts (Have you ever even attempted to talk to a singer-songwriter without it getting flirty? It's utterly impossible) in which I clearly stated I had a boyfriend I loved. Instead of coming clean about his snooping that same night, Panera let his jealousy and suspicions fester until he had convinced himself I was definitely going to cheat on him. The only thing is . . . I was *never* going to cheat on him, and, up until that point, he was actually the only boyfriend I had maintained a sexual attraction to for the duration of the relationship. The only person doing any cheating in that instance was Panera, in that he was cheating himself out of a relationship with a chick who really fucking loved him.

The bottom line is, we all have little secrets, small naughty allowances we give ourselves that don't hurt the ones we love. We all should have little secrets. Little secrets are good—they make us feel alive and give us something that is ours alone in a relationship where many things are shared. If you suspect your partner has a secret that's not so little, ask him or her about it immediately. You are not Inspector Gadget. You don't need to try to handle this one yourself.

Faking Orgasms

Don't do it.

I wish I could end this passage there, but I feel like in this age the millennials reading will probably demand an explanation. As you should. But let me save you some time: under all circumstances, you must always demand an orgasm.

I have never faked an orgasm. Everyone accuses me of lying when I say this, and it pisses me off because there are way more important things to lie about—e.g., how many times I've eaten at Taco Bell this month—but in this case I am not lying. As far as little white sex lies go ("No, it's not that small!"), I think faking an orgasm is the worst for one very simple reason: it tells your partner they are doing the correct thing to please you when they are not. Your pleasure isn't something to be taken lightly in any part of your life and in bed is no different. Sure, there are times to suck it up out of courtesy, like when a friend makes you a dinner that tastes like unseasoned donkey balls, but *nothing about the most intimate act should ever feel like a courtesy*. If you keep that very important line running through your head during every sexual experience, I promise you will always feel satisfied and you will never feel objectified. Even—make that *especially*—during a one-night stand, faking an orgasm shouldn't be an option, if only as an act of kindness to the next person. I don't believe in "participation awards" for people over the age of ten, so please, no fake cumming.

With all that in mind, it's important to acknowledge that fake orgasms aren't always to make our partners feel better—sometimes they're to make us feel better. Women who have trouble reaching orgasm are often embarrassed by it because it's been reinforced so many times that when something on our bodies doesn't look or work in the commercial way, it must mean we're not sexy and it must be our fault. Man, that could really stress some bitches out. Thus, lack of orgasm.

I really had no idea what the fuck an orgasm was beyond theory until I was eighteen and in college. And, honestly, that's a perfectly reasonable time to find out because it's good to have that eighteen-year lead when you can get some work done. The first several years after your first orgasm will be pretty much dedicated to having more orgasms, so please plan accordingly. One of the most common complaints I hear from women is that they can't cum at all or they can't cum with a partner—the first is unacceptable, the second might be some sort of blessing or sign from the cosmos, but I hear you.

If you can't cum solo, you might not know how to properly masturbate. Good thing the Internet exists! Just like I learned how to give a pretty decent blow job from reading about it on the Internet (not watching porn—very important), you can learn how to properly masturbate from the Internet as well. It doesn't matter how old you are, you might just not be doing it right. And, hey, no day like today! When you Google "how to masturbate properly for a woman" a lot of shit comes up. At first that made me a little bit happy and then it made me a little bit sad. At a young age, I understood the concept of male masturbation. I hadn't seen it executed in real life, but I had watched enough movies and heard enough jokes that I could definitely emulate it had you given me a stuffed animal with a cock. Female masturbation? I mean . . . just no clue. I did not even masturbate until I had sex, and even then I had the luxury of being taught how to masturbate by my boyfriend, who was almost a decade older than me and actually knew what he was talking about. The good news is there now seems to be a lot of free information about it readily available on the Internet, including a site called Scarleteen, which describes itself as "sex ed for the real world," and I'll just ignore the part where the title makes me think of the book *The Scarlet Letter*, which, um, kind of has a different meaning. On the website, a young person asks how to masturbate, and the site's founder, Heather Corinna, responds with this list of options for anyone with a vulva and an interest in self-stimulation (raises my hand):

* massaging the clitoral shaft or hood, labia, or mons with hands (either whole hands or with fingers, knuckles, or palms with varying kinds of speed, pressure, or movement) or an object

* rubbing or rocking the vulva up against objects (like a pillow, the edge of a chair, or the edge of the bed)

* inserting fingers or sex toys into the vagina or anus, often paired with clitoral stimulation

* using a vibrator or other toys to stimulate the clitoris, labia, thighs, perineum, rectum, or other sites

* using a faucet or showerhead for clitoral stimulation

* sitting on large vibrating objects, like a washing machine

* pressing and unpressing the thighs tightly together*

I'm telling you, I'm thirty-one and I think I'm going to be referring to this website time and time again. Sex education doesn't need to be—nor should it be—erotic; it just needs to be accepting, inclusive, and informative. If it makes you feel weird to learn about masturbation from a stranger online, ask a friend. If you feel weird asking a friend, get a new friend!

---

* Heather Corinna, "How Do You Masturbate?," Scarleteen, August 31, 2008, http://www.scarleteen.com/article/bodies/how_do_you_masturbate.

Hopefully after visiting that Scarleteen website, you can make yourself howl, but if you can't, check in with your brain. Are you feeling depressed or angry? Those two emotions can really stunt operations down undah. When I'm depressed, I can't even think about masturbating, never mind cumming. Always remember, to have a healthy sex life you yourself should be healthy first. And although it is many times overlooked, this includes mental health.

Before having a complete meltdown because you now can make yourself cum but you can't orgasm with a partner and you think your vag is all fucked up, ask yourself these questions:

1. Am I truly attracted to my partner?

2. Do I feel safe with my partner?

3. Does my partner identify as the gender/have the genitalia that arouses me sexually?

4. Do I feel well? Physically and mentally?

5. Am I focusing on only sex when I have sex or am I letting outside stimuli steal my attention? In other words, am I present?

6. (At the time of sex:) Do I want to be having sex right now?

7. Do I love myself and feel I am deserving of pleasure without shame?

8. Do I know how to properly have an orgasm? (Can I feel it coming? Do I know how to "ride the wave" of the orgasm? Am I comfortable truly releasing in front of my partner?)

9. Am I allowing myself to be vulnerable?

10. Am I insecure about how long I think it's going to take me to cum?

If you feel like you've "tried everything," I highly recommend speaking to your ob-gyn. Any legit pussy doctor takes your sexual satisfaction into account. That's how I knew, when I met my current ob-gyn, I had truly found "the one." My previous doctor, although a woman, was pretty whack. Besides being obsessed with trying to get me to have those HPV shots as soon as they hit the market, she also implied I was an alcoholic when I complained that I felt bloated all the time (I was actually just severely lactose intolerant, which my BFF, Paula, ultimately figured out for me), never asked if I experienced pleasure during intercourse, and thought it was cray that I was coming in at eighteen not wanting kids (I still don't want kids, still get shocked responses, just not from my gyno). So when I first walked into my current ob-gyn's office and had to fill out paperwork that asked me questions like "On a scale of one to five, what is sexual pleasure like for you?" I felt like a goddamn gospel choir was singing behind me. Finally, a medical lady who cared about more than just checking my body for cancer and reminding me that my biological clock is, has been, and will always be ticking.

If your ob-gyn is not asking you questions that cater to your pleasure as well as to your pain, maybe she or he is not the right fit for you. No matter how many diplomas someone has on their office wall, if you don't feel comfortable asking your doctor the same questions you would ask WebMD, their education is not doing you any good. If your doctor gets embarrassed or grossed out by a question you ask, the problem is theirs, not yours. I mean, unless you're just being obnoxious or a fucking idiot. Doctors are people too. To sum it all up, a faked orgasm is a disservice to all parties involved—you don't experience pleasure, your partner has bad habits reinforced, and you're leaving your partner's next partner with more of a mess to clean up. Live by one of my favorite Girl Scout maxims: always leave a ~~place~~ dick better than you found it.

Expecting Your Partner to Be a Mind Reader

Almost every time someone asks Krystyna or me for relationship advice, we respond with "Have you talked to your partner about this?" and almost every single time the person so eager for our opinions sheepishly says no. I sigh, roll my eyes, and sassily reprimand them. Relationships are work, and I cannot do that work for you. By your late twenties and certainly anything beyond that, you're probably a fucking mess. You're the product of all the crap choices you've previously made, horrible folks you've previously dated, and hours you've spent thinking alone—eek!

By the time you're official with someone, I hope they know things about you, like how you take your coffee, the general location of your place of work, and the names of your parents, but getting to truly know the nooks and crannies of a person can and should take years. And wouldn't you know it, the way to get to know a person is through communicating directly with them. Obviously, as a couple you should continue to share stories about your lives for pleasure, but many times information surfaces on a need-to-know basis. So when your heart or your brain starts wondering about something that will potentially affect your partner, instead of guessing what their reaction will be, talk about it. It may be uncomfortable, it may even give you anxiety, and, hell, you might not even get the answer you hoped for, but at least you will know. And as the saying goes, knowing is half the battle.

What's the reason for our phobia of having an intimate conversation with the people who arguably, besides our pets, hear us fart the most? For me, it sometimes seems like I'm embarrassed by my own feelings, but that's not precisely it. I'm very comfortable with the things I feel. I am just uncomfortable sharing them because I distrust how others might handle them. There is also this perplexing notion that releasing my personal hopes, desires, and sexual fantasies spoils them in some way. They lose value. Talking about them is the verbal equivalent of opening a fresh bottle of Diet Coke—after that initial cap turn, it'll never be quite that fizzy again.

While we're chatting about secrets, I have a little secret to share with you: I hate communicating verbally. I really, really hate it. Often I feel like it's meaningless. Even while writing this book, and I love writing, I've stopped multiple times to be like "Jesus, who cares? They get the point." I am in a career where I am constantly surrounded by so many strong opinions that they all become weak. My hatred of speaking wouldn't be as problematic if I hadn't chosen to speak for a living. Between stand-up and podcasting, at the end of the day, when I come home to my boyfriend, I am talked out. This causes problems because, well, he apparently enjoys talking to me.

I haven't always been bad at communicating. As a toddler, I would sit in the front of the shopping cart at the grocery store, waving at people and saying hello on repeat until I received some sort of response. I have a theory that in me existed a talking quota that I reached way too soon. One day I completely shut down.

You would think this is the part where I do the big reveal. I tell you I shut down because a trusted family friend touched my baby vagina and made me promise never to tell or someone at school punched me right in the yapper after I made an announcement on the playground, but none of these things happened. One day I just decided to be the goth being I was put on this planet to be. The world didn't really get me, and as punishment, I ceased sharing myself with the world.

Then, at the approximate age of six, I discovered the beauty of *theatrics*. Why verbalize one's emotions when one can perform them?

This resulted in years of faking injuries at birthday parties instead of saying "I want to go home," and pretending to be stuck in a miniature golf course hole instead of just saying "I'd rather not." It culminated in the most extreme performance of my dramatic diversions and non-communication tactics some years later when I was babysitting my younger brother. I was about twelve, which would make Christopher seven. Chris was bathing, and for the record, really taking his damn time. The kid loved to push my buttons, but I needed him dry and in pajamas by the time Mom and Dad came home. Instead of reasoning with a mere child through actual words, I decided to force him out of the tub using fear. Yes, please get the sister of the year award polished and ready to be presented because in my final production of *Words Are for Peasants* I faked a burglary on my own home. This was by far the most advanced of my works because I, a singular actor, had to play two roles: the burglar and myself. Mostly using the technique of sound effects, I was able to convince little bro that our private space was being invaded. Using my Payless imitation Timberland work boots, I stomped through the entryway, responding to my own footsteps with "Ohmigod!" and "No!" The grand finale was me actually breaking a pane of glass on our front door. And, with a crash, my pruned brother emerged naked from the bathtub. Sometimes victory comes with a cost. For me, the cost was the eight-dollar pane of glass my mother made me buy with my own money, after explaining to the glass proprietor what I had done. In retrospect, this incident was probably mildly scarring, and thank goodness we got this book deal so I can gift Chris some therapy should he need it.

As the curtain fell on my final performance (my mom still has a scar on her arm from cleaning up the glass), I figured out I should probably find a more formal and structured way of expressing myself, but my overall attitude did not and has not really changed. I'm still much better at writing out my feelings than talking them out. My purpose in sharing this is to depict how idiotic it is when we act out instead of speak out. And while you probably haven't faked a burglary to get out of a relationship because you're not Meg Ryan and your life is not a rom-com, you've most likely acted out your displeasure with a relationship rather than verbalizing it. No matter how well someone knows you, and even if they have the capability to know what you need without you saying it, that is not their responsibility. Whether you write it or speak it, you have to tell your partner what you want, what you need, what you like, and what you don't like, because, as a meme I shared on my Instagram once informed me, "what you allow is what will continue." Sometimes memes do get it right (but mostly they're slut-shaming, racist, or riddled with obvious spelling errors).

Stalking the Ex

I'm going to call this one the *Frozen* rule because you need to fucking let it go, and it's a two-parter. When I say "ex" I am simultaneously referring to both your ex-partner and your current partner's ex-partner.

YOUR CURRENT PARTNER'S EX

This is the creepier and more illogical habit, so hopefully it'll be easier to kick. I am fascinated by the ex-girlfriends of my boyfriends. I love hearing all about them because I find them to be video game cheat codes that allow me to enter a relationship at a more advanced level rather than pressing PLAYER ONE START. Most times this has worked out for me because I'm pretty good at listening to and retaining information. I store and archive tales of past loves, which are often exchanged in the first several months of dating, as a sort of Dewey Decimal System for myself. I often refer back to it throughout the course of my relationship to determine how my partner will react to something or as insight into how his mind works. Why waste the hard work another girl has already put in by being so stubborn that I must experience for myself every flaw my new boyfriend has when I can skip ahead and simply uncover previously buried flaws?

I've learned a lot about the loves of my life through these stories. They are almost relationship fables for me. I've gone so far as to become a fan of my boyfriend's exes due to heroic feats endured during their relationship, sassy comments, and current online presences. I always put a feather in my own hat when my boyfriend's résumé includes a lot of intelligent, fiery babes. Most men have a type, and it makes me happy when the woman who came before me was someone spectacular, because one would assume the next person is only going to be that much more spectacular. Sometimes, however, this can go too far. I can begin to think my partner's ex was perhaps "too" spectacular. Especially if she was the one who dumped him, and especially if her legacy seems to surface even after several months with me. I don't want my partner's ex to be garbage, but I also don't want them to be unbeatable, which is tricky in a world of Instagram filters and that flashing light thing you can put on your phone like you're Kim Kardashian.

After you've gotten the gist of the ex, you must separate yourself from her just as she has, hopefully, separated herself from your current partner. Maybe she's lost weight, maybe she's gained weight, maybe she has a new boyfriend, maybe she has a super cute new haircut, maybe she wrote a new joke about feminism that's, like, really fucking good and you can't believe you talk about feminism all fucking day but never even thought to approach it from that angle, but hush, little girlfriend. It's time to ruin your new boyfriend's life in your own unique way. C'mon, you can do it. You're a fucking nightmare!

YOUR EX-PARTNER

I would be lying if I were to sit here naked-bottomed in this SVA sweatshirt and tell you I don't still occasionally look at my ex's social media. Sometimes it's a necessity (I tell myself). Like when I think we might end up at the same comedy event or if I have a feeling he might've gotten engaged or if I'm drinking or if it's a Sunday. But real talk: there was a period of time when I looked at Panera's Instagram, Facebook, and Twitter every day, multiple times a day—a torture I wouldn't inflict on any foe. To quote my relationship guru, Alanis Morissette, once more, "I'm sorry to myself / For treating me worse than I would anybody else."

It's so easy to say it now, but I promise you there is nothing but heartache to gain from continuing to follow your ex on social media. This doesn't mean you cannot eventually be friendly again, but after the breakup there needs to be a clean break of at least several months. That's why the word "break" is in there. For your mental health, you both need a pause. Take it. You will never regret taking it, but you definitely will regret not taking it. After my last breakup, months of my life were spent grasping at something that was never and should never be patched up. It almost killed me. I lost twenty pounds in a little over a month, my tongue turned gray from malnourishment, and my hair began to fall out because I wasn't sleeping or ingesting the proper vitamins, and yet we still continued to text and call and subtweet, and—worst of all—have very intense sex fueled by manipulation, control, and desperation.

But just as quickly as I had downward-spiraled, the day he ignored the fabulous ass shot I had sent him and, when pressured, told me he could not "fuck and watch SNL" because he was "seeing someone," I was released from the prison I had built for myself. Pretty much instantaneously I stopped stalking him online, I stopped contacting him, I stopped thinking about him so much. The minute he was able to choose someone else over me, I knew I had no power anymore. My reign as the most important woman in his life had ended, and I was free. In the future, instead of waiting until a woman I've never met unknowingly emancipates me by replacing me, I will leave with my head held high and of my own accord. I cannot express to you how much time and pain you will save yourself by doing the same. Unfollow. Unfriend. Block. Lose his number. Before you lose yourself in the process.

CORINNE

Breakups

Barring tragedy, breakups are some of the roughest times a person will go through in their lifetime. It's no coincidence the best albums, movies, and classic literature are about romances that for some reason or another didn't ultimately work out. While every breakup is painfully unique, misery does love company, and pity parties are better when more than one person is invited. I've spent hundreds of hours thinking about my breakups—not just why they happened but also why they affected me on such a deep level. Codependency and fear of being alone are common reasons for folks to go off the deep end as they go it alone, but sometimes it's deeper than that.

I'm [Medically] Obsessed With You

For a comic, I'm pretty mentally stable. There's no one who's "all there" who gets into this business, but I've had a pretty normal life—grew up in the suburbs of New Jersey, parents still married, little brother a comfortable five years younger than me, dogs adopted from the local pound because we're heroes, fenced-in backyard with a tire swing, sandbox, and plastic log cabin playhouse, been to Disney World multiple times, and never been molested by a relative (*Yahtzee!*). I like to joke that any problems I've had I created for myself, which is pretty much true, except for my delightful companion obsessive-compulsive disorder. OCD is a fun one because it feels totally made up and ridiculous to everyone around you while it simultaneously completely ruins your life. It's like Chinese water torture for the brain.

Now, I don't force myself to take a shower every time I take a shit (although, I mean, sounds nice), bring my own silverware to restaurants, or get Q-tips stuck in my ears, but I've certainly partaken in my share of OCD rituals—light switches, combination locks, and cracks in the sidewalk have all, at one time or another, been the enemy. My OCD is mostly manageable, and I don't talk a lot about it because the compulsions—the only parts people can visually notice—I mostly nipped in the bud years ago. In middle school I started feeling this intense need to touch and tug on my gym combination lock multiple times before I could exit the locker room. I would stay in there so long that I was always the last person on the gymnasium floor. I would constantly flick my bedroom light switches on and off until it "felt right," and I would have to adjust or reposition things before I felt at peace within. I'm all into being weird, but even twelve-year-old Corinne, who used to dress up in costumes and hand out fresh flowers (for no reason) in front of the local movie theater, recognized that this was beyond a quirk. It was an actual problem because it was disrupting the flow of life. Like the little Matilda I am, the next time I was at the Union Public Library, one of my favorite places and refuge to many a delightful misfit, instead of taking out my go-to piece of literature, *Blood Lust: Conversations with Real Vampires,* I opted for some texts that might help me self-diagnose. A few thick books later, I was like "Ah, okay. I have OCD." I wasn't scared or sad. I was simply relieved I had figured out that the way my mind was treating me was not healthy and I could enjoy a higher quality of life if I just constantly reminded myself that those thoughts weren't normal. That is, my mother wasn't going to die if I didn't turn the key to our house's front door six even times. Furthermore, if she coincidentally died that day, it was in no way related to me turning or not turning the key in that door. Looking back, I'm honestly kind of impressed that in middle school I was able to not only figure out that my behavior was irrational but also actually pinpoint what it was. Books, man—go figure!

While a book was able to help me almost completely conquer my compulsions (the sound switch on the side of the iPhone can still stir up some compulsive behavior in me if I'm particularly anxious before going to bed or sitting down in a movie theater), I went on for many years without realizing the full power of my obsessions. I can get obsessed with anything. Thankfully, I'm also extremely strict with myself, so I would never allow myself to travel down the slippery slope of alcoholism or drug abuse, but I certainly get where those people are coming from. I understand the desire to keep going, to not let the party end, to push yourself that one step beyond your breaking point. As I've mentioned many times on the podcast, I think every person has a column of shit they can deal with in a potential partner and a column of things they don't fuck with. For many people, addiction is a huge no-no. For me, while it's not a check in the pros column, it by no means makes someone off-limits for me, because it's a concept I understand and can cope with.

I'm definitely addicted to food. I often gravitate toward men who are a little chubby or used to be fat because I feel like they just understand me better. It's not even something I specifically look for. It just happens. The Fates bring us fat fucks together. Just the other day a comic friend of mine said, "Wow, there's a little fat kid stuck inside that body of yours." It's true. My soul is basically in a tug-of-war between obsession (which usually leads to overindulgence of something) and strictness (which usually leads to me not allowing myself something). On paper, it sounds a lot worse than it is. And while it's my Achilles' heel, it's also 100 percent the reason for my success.

This is not a book on mental health, really, so it's strange that I spent this long talking about me putzing around with Master Locks, but my lifelong "struggle" with OCD (it wasn't—just more of a looming thing in my life) really came to a head when Panera dumped me. I know everyone thinks their breakup was the worst breakup, but I would like to nominate myself as a front-runner—not because of how he handled it (which was terrible), but because of how I did (which was far worse). Yes, it's shitty to dump your girlfriend of two years in a sandwich shop, never mind a chain sandwich shop. And, yes, it's even shittier to do it after allowing her to pay for your You Pick Two combo. And, yes, it makes it hurt so much more that this was not very long after telling me I was "the one" and writing me letters every day I was on a Birthright Israel trip. These things all suck, but what sucks the most is how poorly I acted for the following, um, twelve months (I'm being generous with myself—it was much longer).

I had gone through breakups before but none that stuck (er, stick) with me in the way the Panera one did (does). Truthfully, I still think about it almost every day, but again, that's my fault because I literally have made a career off it. I had a rocky break from my first boyfriend, Jim, which included a failed open-relationship portion, a controlling portion, and then years of a weird way-too-close-friendship portion. Jim had truly become my best friend by the time I realized I had outgrown him. He was what I lovingly refer to as my training-bra boyfriend—he was my first, I will always feel nostalgic at the mention of his name, but he simply doesn't fit anymore. I wore him until the elastics dried out and snapped, and I still miss his friendship to this day, but we cut it off for good a few years ago after a night out with friends. He tried to initiate sex, I turned him down . . . and that was that.

In contrast, I felt physically ill the day Panera broke up with me. I called in sick to work. I wore leggings and a Victoria's Secret half sweat-shirt to bed. It was a real fucking nightmare. The first stage was coming to terms with how someone could break up with a gal like me. Since Panera seemed unwilling to meet with my personal team of psychologists and one acupuncturist, I was forced to investigate this situation for myself. It was completely on me to figure out what the problem was. I mean, who doesn't like a partner who refuses to talk about feelings, hates all your friends (they were all improv comedians—I rest my case), thinks the comedy theater you perform at is a front for a Scientology-level cult (I still believe this part), and gets annoyed at you when you drop things (he did not have Huntington's disease, to my knowledge)? So, yeah, perhaps I hold people to "impossible standards," but is that not my prerogative? As I said to him many times, "If you don't like it, fucking leave me . . ."

And as I learned, if you say that to a person enough times, no matter how meek the person is, they will do so. It's a good thing to know. Very handy. Before I go any further, I would like to state for the record that I am not a person who should be in *any* relationship. Not because I need more time to work on myself. Not because I need therapy. Not because I need to fuck around. Simply because relationships are not for everyone. Honestly, I think relationships are for mostly nobody, but, well, that's an argument I probably won't win so why bother starting it (and other things I learned on Facebook). By now you've probably started wondering if I'm drinking, and, yes, dear god, I am.

Most of the time I really liked being in a relationship with Panera. Unfortunately, I think the biggest reason was because Panera really liked me. And, well, that wasn't fair to him. The thing is, I think Panera is wonderful. Is. I still do. Yes, obviously I get drunk and go to his Twitter and mentally mock him because I'm a fucking human, but I really do think he's swell. He's talented, he rocks the shit out of a beard, he works hard, he knows the joy of eating beyond one's capacity, and he's simply horrendous with money—qualities I truly respect in a man. But most of all, he believed in me. We'll get back to this later because now I'm drunk crying.

Panera dumped me a little over a month before my twenty-seventh birthday. Unable to fathom going through such a special day without the person I thought I was going to marry (me, a person who never even dreamed of getting married), the night before my birthday I begged him to come over. I honestly cannot believe my behavior. Never before and never again would I act like this, but something so powerful came over me during that breakup. I lost control like I never had before. I had no direction. I felt sad. I felt confused. I felt like I had hit rock bottom. Not just because Panera had left me but because I was kind of left with nothing. My career was going okay. My apartment was okay. My life was okay. But okay is not enough.

In my quest for perfection, my OCD often acts up because it coaxes me into continually replaying every important (or what I categorize as important, which is many times insignificant to others) instance or interaction in my life. As you can imagine, this becomes mentally and physically exhausting pretty quickly. My mind deals with problems the same way a rat navigates a labyrinth: frantically trying new directions until it can find an exit. The only catch is, with OCD, there is no exit. There is no correct and definitive answer, only other endless possibilities that I have yet to think about in an infinity loop until I just resolve to take a nap, because then at least my mind can take a breather.

While my OCD still plagues me, especially when I'm waiting on important news or nervous about something, I don't think it will ever be able to overtake my mind and body again. The good thing about OCD is that while the obsessions and compulsions are illogical, I can talk myself out of some of the behavior through actual logic—a beautiful metaphor for many things in life if ever I saw one.

I'm looking into cognitive behavioral therapy to untrain the trickier parts of my brain, but in the meantime, I know a relationship will never be able to break me in the same way that the breakup heard 'round the world did because my heart isn't built that way anymore, and I find that to be a little bit sad and a little bit comforting. In the meantime, while being dumped will probably always blindside the victim, you can do your part to soften the blow when you're the one dealing out rejection.

How to Dump Someone

We've all been there. It's just not working for you. On the one hand, once you've decided you want to be an active part of a committed relationship, you shouldn't attempt to flee at the first thing that displeases you, but on the other hand, you also shouldn't stay too long after something consistently does . . . *and you've mentioned it to your partner at least three times.* Obviously, there are things—like physical and emotional abuse or cheating—that are grounds for immediate dismissal, but beyond the extremes, if you've decided that you truly love someone and care about their well-being, you need to promise to try to love them without conditions. Loving someone means loving all of them, even the parts you don't love. Does that make sense? Not really, but that's why love is tricky.

Once you've pondered a departure, written up that pros-and-cons list, discussed it at length with your friends, and made the decision that you want to end it, you should make the cut as clean as possible—for the sake of you and for the sake of your soon-to-be-former boo. There is no better time to put into play a saying we've all heard since grade school: treat others the way you would want to be treated.

No one "wants" to get dumped. Even when both parties can agree things need to come to an end, being the one dumped instead of the dumper feels like losing. However, pulling the Band-Aid off quickly and completely can really help the inevitable wound start to heal faster.

Here are some quick tips for a dirty job we've all done or will probably have to do at some time in our lives:

1. **Pick a Safe Space.** There are few millennial phrases that make me roll my eyes harder than "safe space," but if there's any time for one, make it during your breakup. No one likes to bawl their eyes out in a fucking diner, at a crowded movie theater, or during a family function, so for the love of the Spice Girls, do some

location scouting! I always like getting broken up with on my own turf because I feel less vulnerable, I can get into my full-on ugly cry right away, and I can maintain what little shred of dignity I have left by giving the door a powerful slam on the dude's way out. Dumpers often try to choose "neutral" locations where the dumpees will be too embarrassed to act out emotionally, but that's selfish. Unless you think your insignificant other is going to attempt to murder you upon hearing the news that they just became single, take one for the almost-disassembled team that was you guys and hurt them at home.

2. **Don't Brothers Grimm.** Every relationship, once it gets semi-serious, comes with a calendar, which sometimes makes breaking up a constant game of checking your appointments. As nice as it is of you to not break up with someone the day before their sister's wedding (don't you *dare* fucking do that, I don't care how expensive the shit on her registry is), what's also nice of you is to not tell fairy tales to the person you plan on dumping. For instance, if you know you're going to dump someone days after being their plus-one at a wedding, please don't make cutesy chit-chat about what song you guys will come out to as a newlywed couple. If you think the song would be Wilco's "I Am Trying to Break Your Heart" and your almost-ex thinks it would be Whitney Houston's "Greatest Love of All," that little cocktail game is going to come off as just plain rude and make the upcoming sting that much . . . stingier.

3. **Be Clear.** Breakups are shit. Vague breakups are shittier. Yes, sometimes a short separation or a few days to think some things over solo can really help, but those are rare special occasions. Most times a dumper will be vague in breaking up with someone if they're not happy but also not positively sure they can find someone better. If you expect someone to wait on the bench

for you while you go out and talent scout for better ballplayers, you're the asshole and you should feel lucky you've been able to hide that from your patient partner for so long.

4. **Be Honest.** This one can be hard to do, but it can also be the most educational for each side of the equation. Hell, I still have some relationships I was released from in which I know I must've done something "wrong" but I still don't know what that thing was because no one ever had the guts to tell me. And *that thing I maybe did or did not do or should've done* is the thing that keeps me up at night, not the memory of the fella. As a dumper, being honest will give you a lesson in verbalizing what you like, don't like, and need from a partner, and as a dumpee it will give you a hand mirror to self-reflect for a second. Please note, just because *you* didn't like a particular quality in a person or a way they handled a situation doesn't make them incorrect; it merely makes you incompatible. It will give the dumpee the opportunity to think *Hmm, this is something negative about me that I can work on changing to become a better partner.* Or it can let them know that you're a fucking nitpicky psychopath and they just dodged a bullet.

5. **Remember This Is Your Almost-Ex, Not Your Priest.** While honestly vocalizing why things must come to an end from your perspective, your breakup should not be an opportunity for you to air every transgression you've committed throughout the course of the relationship. If you cheated one time six months ago but your infidelity has nothing to do with why you're ending things (and, more likely, the reason you cheated is the reason you're ultimately leaving the relationship), do us all a favor and shut the fuck up. The close of every relationship already comes equipped with that gnawing feeling of *What the fuck did I just do with the past X years of my life?* so it's not necessary to add on the pain

of a large chunk of that time being a lie. If you feel there are things you simply must confess, pen an anonymous postcard to PostSecret, scribble your sins on a scrap of paper and stick it in a crack in the Wailing Wall next time you're in Israel, or tell a therapist. Just don't use your breakup as an opportunity to shed all your guilt. You guys are separated and don't have to—and shouldn't—bear the weight of each other any longer.

had an abortion

I dig the rape fantasy even after I've been raped?

Was this rape?

My city won't test my rape kit...or anyone else's.

My boyfriend is an alcoholic and tried to kill himself and we've only been dating for two months.

lady faked needing an ortion to preach at me!

Is it still rape if you have no emotional distress from it? does that make me a monster?

Empowered pole dancing feminist, but still bulimic

ug addict edophile.

Breaking off relationship with alcoholic mother

I want to rape a girl

Male Rape

Alone, scared, need abortion.

PRO-ABORTION and I have no shame!

2 abortions and affai with married boss

ash backs of my rape ned sex last night

While you left me to do drugs, I fucked some people. Do I tell him or not.

SHIT! Was I molested?

His Dick Has a Condom Phobia

Adoption or abortion

IF I BUY YOU PLAN B LATER CAN I JUST FINISH WITHOUT THE CONDOM?

he forward in ssault case ocal coach?

SAFE SEX AND SERIOUS STUFF

Condoms su

Blackout sex explain?

ating a Horrible Man for Her Safety!

I've been raped an

Psychotic on birth control

My brother might be a pedophile and I can't stop hating him

Birth control made me SUICIDAL/ copper IUD saved me

Obsessed Over Safe Sex My Whole Life and Still Got Slapped With the Herpes Stick

My birth control is $162?!?!

I took the test and knew I was going

ile?

birth control is ruining my fucking life

I think I was sexually assaulted at a Halloween party please help

RGENT PLEASE FOR THE LOVE OF GOD EVEN THO M AN ATHEIST: I AM PREGNANT AND THIS FUCKING OUNTRY DOESN'T ALLOW ABORTIONS AND I AM URRENTLY ALWAYS MID FAINT BECAUSE OF THAT.

In Texas, Abstinence-Only Programs May Contribute To Teen Pregnancies

My Best Frien Should Tell M About My Abc

Pregnant & addicted to porn

he took the condo when I wasn't loo

My best friend's boyfriend sexually assaulted me. H3LP!

Is my husband a pedophile?

old My Mother t My Assault

I Was Molested and My Parents Never Told Me

Male birth control - are men the weaker sex?

Should I come forward in the sexual assault case against my vocal coach?

My Best Friend Thinks I Should Tell My BoyFriend About My Abortions

Dating a "recovering" drug addict and almost marrying a Pedophile.

Sugar Daddy date turne Asphyxiation Session

I have HIV, you don't have HIV

Is it normal for your husband to be "mildly" verbally abusive?

I'm scared I will become a pedophile, or that I already am one

If there's one thing we've learned from hosting *Guys We Fucked,* it's that being silent about socially taboo subjects is futile. The more we shared about our sex lives and the sex lives of our guests, the more people felt the need to divulge their personal experiences to us, specifically the traumatic ones. Initially, it was confusing. Why would a person e-mail two strangers he or she or they listens to on the Internet and talk about, at great length, extremely dark and traumatic instances of assault they experienced? The majority of these e-mails included the sentence "You are the only people I've ever told about this." This was the biggest shocker, since neither of us has experienced sexual assault, so it wasn't like we were coming from a place of being in similar shoes. Once we started to receive an average of two "I was raped" or "I was molested" e-mails per day, it became clear that this is a much bigger problem than we realized. Our inbox has become an authentic glimpse of what people are actually thinking and feeling about sex, and it's vulnerable and tragic and human. The best and most beautiful part—not to get all Oprah on you guys—is it's bullshit-free. It's crazy that hundreds of thousands of strangers are willing to open up to us instead of opening up to their spouses, close friends, or therapists, but given all the ways society tries to convince us that we're not good enough, it's no wonder people have a guard up and keep their pain to themselves. A newly realized goal of the podcast is to let people know that it's okay to talk about the bad stuff. In fact, it's profoundly important for both yourself and others who are living with the same type of shame but are convinced they're alone in their thinking. We're all fucked up in one way or another, so let's just agree to cut the bullshit and start talking about this.

Sex Ed

Krystyna

In the United States, public schools are required to teach some form of sex education. The depressing part is that a school can choose to implement an abstinence-only curriculum, and according to many reputable studies and, ya know, logic . . . that shit does not work. It's one of the reasons why the United States ranks number one in developed countries as having the highest teen pregnancy rate.[*] Telling hormonal teenagers to "Just say no" to sex, as if someone is trying to tempt them with a crack pipe at a party, is a disservice to their education. If the kids want to fuck, the kids are gonna fuck. And if no one teaches them about safe sex, then guess who's going raw dog at Brittany's party full of underage drunk hornballs who just tried vodka for the first time? Sexual desire is a strong force during your teenage years, and it's too easy to act on impulses without thinking of the potential consequences. Especially if you have no idea where those consequences can lead or how they can change your life.

According to a survey done by the Guttmacher Institute, 23 percent of sex education curriculums in U.S. public schools teach absti-

---

[*] K. F. Stanger-Hall and D. W. Hall, "Abstinence-Only Education and Teen Pregnancy Rates: Why We Need Comprehensive Sex Education in the U.S.," *PLoS One* 6, no. 10 (2011): e24658, https://www.ncbi.nlm.nih.gov/pmc/articles/PMC 3194801/.

nence as the only way to avoid pregnancy or STIs.* I mean, technically, yes, not having sex is a pretty foolproof way of avoiding pregnancy and (most) STIs. I don't want to get into a car accident, so does that mean I should avoid getting a driver's license? Hell no. I studied for a written exam and then I had to make very intimidating left turns while a man who looked like Santa Claus stared at me with his clipboard, rolling his eyes as I stalled in the middle of an intersection.

So if our schools aren't teaching safe sex, what *are* they teaching? Well, sorry to say that the U.S. government allots tens of millions of taxpayer dollars each year to teaching kids that premarital sex likely leads to "physical and emotional harm."** You know what's *actually* physically and emotionally harmful? Getting pregnant at fifteen because you don't know how to use a condom. *Or* going the abstinence route and then having to wait years to eventually spend thousands of dollars on a wedding at which you recite a shitty haiku to someone and then have shitty sex after hours of drinking shitty wine coolers while dancing to shitty music, only to discover that you're not sexually compatible, but too bad because you're committed to this person for life now. Woof. I feel emotionally harmed just thinking about that. Schools need to come up with non-scare, factual tactics to keep kids from becoming teen parents. Fact: same-sex intercourse has never led to pregnancy. Tactic for conservative school districts: just tell your students to have gay sex! *Boom.* There's a start.

---

* "Fact Sheet: Induced Abortion in the United States," Guttmacher Institute, January 2017, https://www.guttmacher.org/fact-sheet/induced-abortion-united-states.

** Ephrat Livni, "Study: Abstinence-Only Sex Ed Up," ABC News online, September 26, 2017, http://abcnews.go.com/Health/story?id=117935&page=1.

Things I Wish My School Had Covered in Sex Ed

* Just because a male's orgasm is an integral part of pregnancy does not mean a woman's orgasm is not important or required. Sexual satisfaction for all parties involved is vital, even though that may not involve an orgasm, depending on the person. Anything less than that is just plain rude. Don't be rude. Rude people suck.

* Unless you fuck it seconds after an infected person fucks it, you cannot get an STI from a toilet seat.

* Sexually transmitted infections are extremely common. The best ways to avoid contracting one, aside from abstinence, include the use of male and/or female condoms, dental dams, and lube. Lube is your friend, especially when a butthole is involved.

* Despite what society seems to scream at us by way of our friends and the media, herpes is *not* a scarlet letter. If someone discloses to you that they have herpes, it's foolish to think that means they're careless. On the contrary, they *know* what their STI status is. And that's more than a lot of your future sex partners will be able to offer, since the odds of having an STI without knowing it, because you haven't gotten tested, are higher than you think.

* Judging others based on how much or how little they have sex is stupid and irrelevant, and a reflection of how you feel about yourself. So instead of calling the girl in your social studies class a slut, look in the nearest mirror and ask yourself why you feel the need to put other people down.

* The sex you see in porn and the sex you have in real life are completely different types of sex. For the love of fucking, stay in your lane.

* It's okay to have sex if you want to and feel ready and take the necessary steps to be safe. It's also okay to abstain from sex. You are the only one who is fully capable of making a decision over your body, and if others refuse to respect that, that's on them.

* Sexual organs come in all shapes, sizes, colors, smells, and abilities.

* Magazines trick people into thinking there's only one type of body that emulates physical perfection, and that is one big smelly steaming pile of horseshit.

* A lot of people have been or will be sexually assaulted. For some people, it can happen at an extremely young age. While this can be a traumatic experience for every age and gender, being a victim of sexual assault does not mean you are damaged or at fault. If you've experienced sexual assault, telling a parent, teacher, guidance counselor, or police officer is a good first step toward healing. In the unfortunate event that you're met with skepticism, seek out another person you trust to confide in if possible.

* Masculinity and femininity are tiny imaginary boxes based on narrow-minded ideas of what it means to be a man or a woman. Don't mistake one person's concept of gender as your own.

Krystyna

Smooshmortion (Abortion)

I couldn't write (half) a book on sexuality without talking about abortion. It's a touchy subject for some people, but tough shit. We're going there.

Abortion is an issue I feel extremely passionate about. I've met and spoken with a lot of people about it. People I'm related to. People I'm friends with. People I've encountered at bars or parties. People I've had sex with. And many people who listen to our podcast, a lot of whom are just as passionate as I am, except they believe the exact opposite of what I believe. I get it. I wholeheartedly understand why some people aren't keen on the idea of babies being killed. Survey five strangers the next time you go outside, and odds are, they will all be against babies getting killed.

The branding surrounding the pro-life movement is a big ol' bummer. The word itself sounds like a no-brainer: pro + life = positive things! But when you start to associate it with giant photos of dead fetuses, it gets murky. This is not to say that every pro-life person spends days on end at Kinko's amassing a collection of abortion-fetus photos only to throw them in the faces of scared young women. I know plenty of pro-lifers who don't. That said, if you are reading this book and have made aforementioned trips to Kinko's, please stop.

Before I go any further, here are a few facts about me that I want you to know:

* I've never had an abortion.

* I have had completely unprotected sex with two people in my life. No condoms. No birth control pill or IUD. Just the pull-out method. ("Method" is a poor word choice, by the way. It's more like the complete absence of an actual birth control strategy.)

* I've been on seven different types of birth control since I was sixteen. Four types made my boobs swell so much that I legitimately thought they were on the verge of bursting at all times. Two types gave me atrocious cystic acne that made me not want to leave my house. And all seven types sent me into what I can only describe as psychosis. The birth control ended up making me too mean to have sex with. (I would like to take a moment to apologize to Nathan for screaming *"I hope you get hit by a car tonight and die!!"* after I stormed out of our date at a Brooklyn bowling alley. It wasn't you. But it also wasn't me. It was the pill.)

* I took Plan B once when I was twenty-three, after having unprotected sex with a man I was extremely attracted to and wanted to date so, so, so bad. After telling him, via text message, that I was nervous to take it and scared of what it might do to me mentally and physically, he texted back, "Sorry." I was no longer attracted to him after that. (Cue Cyndi Lauper's "True Colors.")

* I've had close friends who got pregnant unexpectedly and decided to terminate that pregnancy, and I supported their decision 100 percent. I had one friend in the same situation and she wanted to keep the baby because she felt as though abortion was "getting in the way of God" and couldn't bring herself to do it, even though

she did not want to have a baby at that time in her life. I supported her decision 100 percent.

* I am no longer on a birth control pill. Not because I want to get pregnant, but because I don't want to be a raging monster to the people I love. I know that IUDs are an option, and I currently have several pamphlets from different IUD companies on my desk. One of them has a picture of a young girl pretending to play an acoustic guitar on her bed as she looks at the camera. There is a quote above her head that says, and I am not bullshitting you, "Music is *my* baby!!" So . . . definitely not getting that one.

* Stephen and I use condoms every time we have sex. Even when I was on the pill, we used condoms 90 percent of the time because he has a huge fear of getting me pregnant. Most people I tell this to cannot fathom the fact that we use condoms and have been together for six years, but like I said, I don't want to get pregnant. And I respect his paranoia, because condoms can break and I really sucked at taking the pill at the same time every day. I'm going to make a lot of people yell out loud into a room of no one else, but I gotta say, I truly don't mind condoms. I can tell the difference, but I love sex *just* as much with or without one.

* If I were to get pregnant at this point in my life, I don't think I could get an abortion, even though I do not want children for another seven or so years. I've given this a lot of thought.

A male listener e-mailed us once, after hearing me talk about people who are pro-life, and he suggested that I replace that phrase with "anti-choice," which I have ever since. That is exactly what abortion is to me, a choice. A say over the direction of my life and what does or does not happen to my body. In theory, I should be the only person who has a say over my own body, but I'm not. The government has a huge say over my body. A government comprised mostly of people who can't even get pregnant. Who don't have a uterus or a vagina or a menstrual cycle. Who don't have to deal with birth-control-induced psychosis. Abortion is legal in the United States, yet as of 2017, four states have only one clinic where a woman can get an abortion. This is largely due to TRAP laws (Targeted Regulation of Abortion Providers), which aim to shut down clinics where abortions are provided, forcing a large number of women to drive out of state to see a provider, but only if they can afford to make the drive and stay in a hotel for a few nights. There are laws in several states that legally require women to get counseling, go through a twenty-four- to forty-eight-hour mandatory waiting period, and see the ultrasound image of the fetus before getting an abortion. All this after they've already made the decision to not have a child. If they *do* want to have a child—a decision that will alter their life—is the doctor legally required to ask them if they're sure or if they're ready or if they're willing and able to take on the responsibility of another living human? Nah, they'll figure it out!

A lot of states require an abortion clinic to obtain official privileges from the hospital in closest proximity. This is an example of a TRAP law that sounded logical to me upon learning about it, but this is also total anti-choice bullshit disguised as being pro-woman. It is extremely rare that an abortion procedure would require hospitalization. In fact, you have higher odds of needing emergency medical care after getting a penicillin injection or a colonoscopy than you do after getting an abortion. Because hospitalization rates are so low for abortion procedures, hospitals will often not grant clinics the required privileges they need, forcing that clinic to shut its doors. *Le sigh.*

I could go on about all the other ludicrous hoops women have to jump through to receive the care we need and deserve and are legally entitled to, but we have a page limit for this book. The thing that really makes my blood boil, and what I think all of these bullshit laws are saying, is that women cannot be trusted to make the right decision for themselves. It's a form of control. I am a competent person, but you wouldn't know that by looking at all the laws keeping me from making decisions about my own sexual organs.

Early on in the podcast, Corinne and I had on a close friend of mine, Audrey, who had just gotten an abortion. She told us about her experience and how traumatic it was to make that decision. The episode was called "Too Late for Plan B, Too Early for an Abortion?" because Audrey went to the doctor during a time when it was just that, and she had to wait a week before she could terminate her pregnancy so the doctors could make sure the fetus wasn't developing in the fallopian tubes, which could be deadly. Since this decision is so personal, I wanted Audrey to speak for herself:

> The decision to have an abortion was the hardest one I've ever faced. While I have no regrets about the choice I made and I know it was the right one, it was a decision I wish I hadn't been faced with. It was one I made after much thought, tears, and emotional turmoil. I'm fortunate enough to live in a place where I was able to make such a difficult, personal decision without the government-imposed barriers many women face in other parts of the country. I'm fortunate to live in a place where I actually had a choice. My unplanned pregnancy is something that would forever change my life, whether I decided for or against an abortion. Every woman should be given the freedom to make this monumental decision without undue influence or hardship placed upon her by those who hold political office.

Ever since we interviewed Audrey, we've been receiving e-mails from women all over the world telling us about their struggle, and often failure, to find the medical care they need to make the decision they want to make. We've also been getting a certain type of e-mail from teenage girls that—after the fourth, fifth, and sixth instance of the same story line—freaks me the fuck out. They're from girls aged thirteen to seventeen whose friend just found out she's pregnant. That friend either cannot afford the fee to cover the abortion or cannot get an abortion because she lives in a state that requires minors to get parental consent. So what do these girls do? They try to abort the baby themselves, and the friend, terrified and desperate, e-mails us asking if we know of any alternative methods or pills or funding or something—anything—that isn't life-threatening. I'll never forget the first time I read one of those e-mails. It was from a sixteen-year-old girl—let's call her Jane—whose best friend just found out she was pregnant. The friend didn't have the money required to cover the cost of an abortion, so she decided to take matters into her own hands in the only way she knew how at that time. She ran around her school's track as fast as she could and started punching herself in the stomach. Unsure if that worked, she went home and chugged half a bottle of vodka. Still unsure, she debated sticking a wire hanger up her uterus, and that's when Jane decided to e-mail us.

I was walking down a New York City sidewalk when I read that e-mail and almost accidentally walked into oncoming traffic. If Corinne and I, two comedians with a sex podcast, are receiving *multiple* e-mails of this nature, that tells me this is happening a lot more than we realize.

We wanted to address this problem on the podcast with a professional, because what the fuck do I know? What do I tell this girl other than "Um, please don't stick a wire hanger up your vagina!!!" Luckily there is an amazing organization called Lady Parts Justice that aims to provide people with knowledge about what's going on in their individual state as far as reproductive rights are concerned. Those women connected us with Dr. Linda Prine, activist, author, and founder and medical director of the Reproductive Health Access Project. She has done extensive research on abortions, provides doctors with the proper training needed to do the procedure, and administers abortions herself, both in NYC and around the country. Dr. Prine cleared up a lot of misconceptions I didn't even know I had about abortions and reproductive health care, and named several resources for women who don't have access to complete reproductive health care.

I wish every sexually active human on the planet could be armed with the accurate knowledge needed to make an informed decision. Here are some facts I've learned about abortion through Dr. Prine and other medical professionals, as well as a few resources that might be helpful to you or someone close to you. Read it. Highlight it. Reference it. Pass it along to a friend in need. If I can prevent one teenage girl from thinking her only option is a wire hanger, then everything I've ever done in my life up until this point will have been worth it.

Abortion Facts (That I Am Sad to Say I Was Totally Clueless on at the Age of Twenty-Eight)

* Getting a legal—thus, safe—abortion does not harm a woman's reproductive organs or her ability to conceive in the future, regardless of how many times she gets the procedure. The same goes for taking the morning-after pill.

* In the United States, women face a higher risk of death from carrying a baby to term than they do from getting a legal abortion.

* There are two options for safe abortions that are equally effective:

Medication Abortion. This method can be used up to ten weeks into a woman's pregnancy and allows her to have an abortion at home, versus in a doctor's office. It consists of two types of pills. The first pill is called mifepristone and causes the pregnancy tissue to detach from the uterus and stop growing. This pill is taken along with antibiotics to avoid infection. The second pill is called misoprostol. Your doctor will instruct you to take these twenty-four to forty-eight hours after the first pill (the time frame will vary per person). These pills can be placed between the teeth and inner cheek and eventually swallowed *or* they can be inserted into the vagina. The vaginal method is not FDA approved, even though it is safe. Three to five hours after the second round of medication, heavy cramping and bleeding start to happen and last for up to four hours. A woman can continue to bleed for nine to sixteen days after that.

Procedural Abortion. This is often referred to as a surgical abortion, which is a misnomer because it doesn't involve surgery or incisions of any kind. There are several different types, depending on how far along the pregnancy is. If a woman is up to sixteen weeks pregnant, she can get an aspiration procedure, during which the doctor uses a small, handheld device called a manual vacuum aspirator. The cervix gets dilated and stretched, and the aspirator is placed up the cervix to remove the pregnancy tissue. This procedure takes about five minutes.

For more info about abortions and organizations that can help with funding and services, see the resources at the back of the book (page 235).

Now, like most of you, I am emotionally exhausted by Donald Trump, but it's imperative that I point out America's current political climate because there is an actual chance that the resources we're including in the book could be majorly fucked in the near future. I'm writing this days after Neil Gorsuch, a staunchly anti-choice judge, was confirmed as a U.S. Supreme Court Justice. The current vice president has made it his personal mission to defund Planned Parenthood in the state he once governed. He even threatened to shut down the government over funding to Planned Parenthood. Oh! And this one time he cosponsored a bill that would take away funding for any women seeking abortions after what he calls "forcible rape." Also known as, ya know, *rape*. To throw a rotting cherry on top of the shit sundae that is the future of women's reproductive rights, our current president's cabinet members make up one of the most anti-choice presidential administrations in modern history. The president has said he will defund Planned Parenthood unless they agree to stop providing abortions. And if you want to add some homeless dog's diarrhea on top of the rotting cherry on top of the shit sundae, I will remind you that same president said that women will let you do anything to them if you're a star, including but not limited to *Grabbing. Them. By. The. Pussy.* So, yeah.

I want there to be fewer abortions in the world just as much as an anti-choice person does, but rallying behind TRAP laws and picketing outside clinics isn't going to get the job done. I could cite studies for this, but it really comes down to common logic. The more information you have, the better you feel about the decisions you make, the more empowered a human becomes. Knowledge is power, and we need to make a stronger effort to ensure that as many people as possible are getting accurate information at a young age about their bodies, sex, sexuality, and how babies are made.

Don't get me wrong—that won't turn abortion into a thing of the past. I haven't even dived into women who seek abortions after being raped or women who want to have a late-term abortion because multiple doctors have confirmed that the child will die during or shortly after birth. Those unfathomable scenarios are still going to occur. But if you feel moved to take action in hopes of lowering the abortion rate, don't aim to take away a woman's choice. Aim to empower her.

Krystyna

When It Comes to Alcohol, Don't Be a Fucking Idiot

Alcohol plays a big role in people's sex lives and can lead to you making choices you wouldn't necessarily make while sober. While being on a substance is absolutely no excuse for taking advantage of another person, we live in a world where it happens constantly. Both Corinne and I have had plenty of drunken or drug-induced sexcapades, and we'll probably continue to have them, but it's important to be responsible with any recreational substance. The first step in responsible sexin' on substances is to *know your limits*.

Drugs affect every person differently. Do you have a friend who is really great when they're sober but the second they have a few drinks they're yelling at you for something you never did five years ago? Are *you* that friend? As you experiment with substances, take note of how they make you feel and how they cause you to act toward others. If I throw back a couple of whiskeys, I'm usually a horny ball of love and sunshine, except when I'm angry or upset over something that is happening in my life. When that's the case, adding alcohol to the equation makes everything ten times worse. My typical lovey-dovey drunk demeanor goes down the tank, and I'm just a sad sack of shit sitting in the corner, beating myself up in my head. That is precisely why I no longer drink while sad or angry. It's not fun for me or those around me, not to mention alcohol is not a healthy coping mechanism. Using it as a social lubricant to enjoy a night out with your friends and possibly hit on a few hotties at the bar? Dope. Relying on it to make you forget about the screaming match you just had with your mom because she's throwing her life down the toilet over a pain pill addiction after your dad left her? Ehhh, that ain't gonna work out so well.

When it comes to sex, alcohol might give you the courage to approach someone and make a move, sure, but have one too many cocktails as you bond over your extensive library of *Seinfeld* quotes and your mutual love of Cool Ranch Doritos, and you could be in for a shitty game of Find the Right Hole. Add to that a rapid spinning sensation and you are fucked, but not the kind that involves good sex. Most people have an easier time getting laid with booze in their system, which is why we associate drinking with hooking up, but that's just the end result. The sexy part of sex rapidly declines the more drinks you knock back. If you really think about it, drinking in order to have sex is pretty fucking dumb. We mask our mediocre personalities with some fun juice in exchange for terrible sex. But guess what? Your mediocre personality will always be there, right underneath that thin layer of intoxication, so work on that first, instead of pushing it down. We're all insecure messes, but that can be fixed by incorporating self-reflection, self-love, honesty, and therapy into your life.

In case you need further proof of alcohol being a bummer in the bedroom, let's consult science. Alcohol is a depressant, so it reduces the functionality of your nervous system, which is, ya know, a pretty important part of fucking someone, unless you have a Gumby fetish. Straight women: Have you ever hooked up with a guy and, as you're removing each other's clothes, he keeps telling you how smoking hot you are and how he can't wait to fuck you, but when the underwear comes off, the raging boner you expect to smile down upon is nowhere to be found? Even after a ton of foreplay and a blow job so good you want to give *yourself* a high five? Some girls, in their drunken state, automatically assume it's their fault, but fuck that noise, because it's not your fault. It's biology's fault! Alcohol increases the level of angiotensin in men, the hormone that causes erectile dysfunction. No blow job technique can reduce the levels of angiotensin in a dude's system. And for women, a few vodka sodas might lubricate your personality, but they do not lubricate your vagina. The dehydration that comes along with alcohol consumption causes vaginal dryness, along with fatigue and headaches. Yum! Who's horny now?!

Imagine if porn stars got wasted before filming a scene. "Seth Wankit and his dehydrated Beanie Baby dick stars alongside Molly McTitFace and her tired desert pussy in the new sexy flick *The Porn Identitty*!" Spoiler alert: it's just twelve minutes of Molly trying to stuff Seth's penis inside her without starting a fire.

If you need copious amounts of alcohol flowing through your veins in order to have sex or have fun with your friends or enjoy a comedy show, stop and ask yourself why that is. Does alcohol give you all of your confidence? Do you feel unattractive when you're sober? Do you dislike yourself? If you answered yes to any of those questions, put down the beer and figure out why.

Consent

SLURRED LINES

Krystyna

Sex and alcohol can really blur the lines of consensual sex. Both Corinne and I have had drunken sex. Fortunately, we've never had a drunken sexual encounter that we've regretted or that's crossed the line into rape territory, but judging by the amount of e-mails we receive about alcohol and unwanted force, and the endless news stories about rape that involve drinking, this is a huge fucking problem, especially at colleges.

It's a very *Tale of Two Cities* time in which to be a woman (both the best and worst of times), but just as we wouldn't take our eyes off our iPhone at a busy bar, we cannot intoxicate ourselves with booze and become blasé about danger, leaving our vaginas unattended. Anything valuable is and will always be ripe for the picking, and while the fault lies entirely on the predators, creeps, and losers who surround us, the power of the knowledge that we can and must protect ourselves rests in our nail-art-adorned hands. No rape is your fault, no matter how much vodka is involved, but we must not forget that the world is still a relatively unsafe place for women, and we, unfortunately, must always be prepared for battle.

Drink Responsibly

If you're a person who blacks out after drinking a certain amount, you've probably experienced those times when your friend or partner fills you in on what you did last night. Blacking out is scary, and it can sometimes lead to sexual encounters you may or may not have wanted.

When someone enters an alcohol-induced blackout, it's because their nerve cells have weakened to the point of no longer being able to store incoming information. Like I mentioned earlier, alcohol is a depressant, and the more you drink, the lower your nervous system's ability to function. Essentially, your brain cells just straight-up stop communicating with one another.* No wonder people have zero memory of what happens during a blackout. Their brain cells took a fucking time-out!

A lot of how our bodies process alcohol has to do with genetics. Other factors include

* how much you ate before you started drinking (never, ever drink on an empty stomach—that's just asking to get tanked fast and feel like shit the next day);

* how alcoholic your drinks are (liquor obviously has a higher amount of alcohol than beer or wine, but liquor paired with a sugary mixer is by far the worst because sugar causes alcohol to be absorbed into your bloodstream at a faster rate); and

* how fast you consume alcoholic beverages (this is the most important one, because if a person drinks three whiskey sours in thirty minutes, they are far more likely to black out compared to

---

* Jim Dryden, "The Biology Behind Alcohol-Induced Blackouts," *The Source*, Washington University in St. Louis, July 6, 2011, https://source.wustl.edu/2011/07/the-biology-behind-alcoholinduced-blackouts.

someone with twice as much alcohol in their blood from drinks consumed over a longer period of time).*

I can't stress this enough: if a person sexually assaults you, I don't give a fuck how much you drank or smoked or snorted. That is *not* okay and that is *not* your fault. I wish we could just say "Don't rape!" and have sexual violence be a thing of the past, but that is not the world we live in. So . . .

The most important question to ask yourself before engaging in drunk sex is

AM I OR IS MY PARTNER TOO DRUNK TO CLEARLY AND ENTHUSIASTICALLY CONSENT TO SEX?

If the answer to that question is yes or even maybe, what should happen next is

NO SEX, NO TOUCHING, NO NOTHING.

If you're unsure what it means to clearly and enthusiastically consent to sex, it's okay. You're not the only one. The "clearly" part means that the person is not slurring their words and speaking like someone who is fully aware and conscious. Apparently, way too many people don't know what the "enthusiastic" part means. Maybe the sex element of the equation is throwing you off. If so, just replace the act of having sex with eating a slice of pizza.

Let's say you and a friend, Rebecca, go on a bar crawl, and at the end of the night you ask Rebecca if she would be interested in going back to your place to enjoy a slice of pepperoni pizza. If Rebecca gives you a clear, vocal "Yes!" and the expression on her face doesn't look as if she'd rather eat grass out of a cow's ass than spend another second

---

* Cathy Zhu, "What Happens to Your Brain When You Black Out?" Greatist.com, September 30, 2015, http://greatist.com/health/what-happens-brain-when-you-black-out.

in your presence, Rebecca has just given you enthusiastic consent. It's important to keep in mind that consent can be revoked at *any* time. Even if Rebecca is sitting at your kitchen table while the pizza heats up in the oven. Even if you're slicing up the pizza and using your mom's china because you think Rebecca is rad and deserves to be served food on fancy-ass mom plates. Maybe Rebecca picks up the slice of pizza, takes two bites, and says, "I don't want pizza anymore." If that's the case, you might assume her stomach hurts or she's full or your pizza fucking sucks, but none of that shit matters because she has every right to change her mind. You would never think to force the slice of pizza down Rebecca's throat. That would be a physically violating and sadistic thing to do to another person.

Similarly, if Rebecca gives you her enthusiastic consent to engage in sex, she has every right to change her mind at any point. Even if her top is off or you're in the middle of putting the condom on, or you're inside her or touching her in any way.

It's important for everyone to be proactive about their own safety and, especially if you're a woman, look out for the safety of other women. I've walked by many wasted dames in NYC who were sitting on the sidewalk, alone, struggling to sit up straight. I always approach them and ask if they need help getting a cab. One or two have told me to go fuck myself, but most have appreciated the help. Here are some other suggestions to help you be more proactive about your personal safety when it comes to drinking:

* Be with people you know and trust.

* Learn how much your body can take.

* Don't drink on an empty stomach.

* Drink a fuck ton of water—it's the difference between waking up feeling like a minivan ran over your body and waking up wanting to get dressed and go out into the world.

* If you notice one of your friends looks majorly fucked up, be a doll
  and get them a goddamn glass of water—or a cab.

Rape

After every live show Corinne and I do, we have at least one person
who approaches us during the meet and greet and tells us they were
raped. One time, after a *Guys We Fucked* tour show, we were saying
hello and taking pictures with a long line of people and I noticed an
older guy, maybe in his early forties, patiently standing alone at the
end of the line. He stuck out because he's not our typical demographic,
especially for the meet-and-greet portion. I remember thinking, *Aw! I
love him!* because he didn't seem fazed by it. A part of me also thought,
Shit, I hope he's not a creeper! but that thought is always casually floating in my head. The line finally dwindled down to just him, and as
we smiled and said hello, his eyes started to water. In a very calm and
quiet voice, the voice of a person who has been through some serious
shit, he said, "I just want to say thank you." We've met thousands of
people after shows, and usually when a person opens with "I just want
to thank you . . ." there is a 99 percent chance they're going to tell us
about something traumatic that has happened. I try to say the right
thing as often as I can, even though I still don't exactly know what the
right thing to say is. When this particular gentleman approached us,
it was one of the few moments when I had no words. He told us that
his teenage daughter was raped a few years ago, and the only reason
she had been able to open up to him about it was because they both
separately listen to the podcast, and after hearing all the stories about
sexual assault, his daughter decided she wanted to confide in him. He
thanked us for making his daughter feel comfortable enough to lean
on him and for bringing them closer as a family. Looking into the eyes
of a father as he tells you this, while tears are streaming down his face,
is a powerful moment you never forget. If every person could feel what

I felt that night, I truly think it could change the world for the better and humanize a problem that is tragically common. Unfortunately, that is next to impossible. So in hopes of shedding light on rape and how intricate people's feelings toward it can get, here is a small chunk of e-mail subject lines with the word "rape" in them, taken verbatim from our inbox:

ANOTHER RAPE EMAIL (it's okay, we're doing good things in the world) (also donald trump is an asshole)

post rape sexuality

How to talk about rape

Was this rape?

Has rape affected my sexual identity?

Flash backs of my rape ruined sex last night

A Rape Survivor's Response to the defenseless Brock Turner

Women should not be punished for being raped.

Mouth Rape

My city won't test my rape kit . . . or anyone else's.

How do you know if you're a victim of rape?!

Male Rape

Trying to profit off a rape

Uncle Sam Wants You (to get away with rape)

That weird gray area of rape we all know and love

Jesus won't slut shame you if it was rape, right?

Rape? Abuse? Did I like it? Can abusive relationships be kinks? help please!!!

Rape in the workplace . . . common or nah?

1 year anniversary! of my rape??

Rape in Greek Life / Am I a bad person?

Female on female rape . . . It's a real thing

man in this article states: god says it's okay to rape your wives? WTF.

Can we have a candid discussion about rape?

My uncle blamed me for raping me when I was 5

Marital rape

I want to rape a girl

I want to rape a girl (update)

I don't know if this counts as rape or not

I FORGIVE The Man That Tried To RAPE Me . . . Is That Wrong?!

Hockey, Rape Threats, Stalking, Ambulances

How Do I Stop Being in Denial About Rape?

When dates get a little rape-y

I dig the rape fantasy even after I've been raped?

I lost my virginity to a girl who accused me of rape after all was said and done

My rape story and request to tell medical professionals: don't assume no condom sex is consensual and be kind!

Line between consensual drunk sex & rape

Finally told parents about my rape

My rape has been less tragic because of you

Forgotten rape

Rape (or is it?) Guilt

Airbnb Rape Story

Where is the rape line?

"you deserve rape"

Raped 2.5 times but my parents don't believe rape is real.

Rape story victory . . . Sort of

Stopped a rape in Hoboken! Should I publicly shame this guy?

Trump's Rape Comments and the BDSM community

How I will stop frat boys from DRUGGING and RAPING

Is it still rape if you have no emotional distress from it? does that
make me a monster?

My Best Friend Committed Suicide After Planning My Rape

Was I raped when I lost my virginity?

The Struggles of Gang Rape

Best Friend of 7 years Rapes other Best Friend (Both Girls)

Roommate and my brother rape?

Did I Rape Him?

Why lie about rape?

Potential rape (or something of that nature) that I avoided because
of you guys.

My Boyfriend Handled My Rape Way Too Well

How to Be Good at Being Raped, i.e.,
What You Should Do If You Were Raped

Ashley, a previous podcast guest and victim of sexual assault, once
told us, after we asked her what people should do after being raped,
"Well, if you're a superhero, then you should go to the cops." There's

no "right" way to react after something traumatic happens. Maybe you're in shock and can't form sentences. Maybe you feel broken. Maybe you're totally okay. Maybe you're confused. Maybe you're bothered by the fact that you're *not* bothered by it. I can't stress this enough: if you don't emotionally have it in you to go to the police or the ER, that is understandable. If you can't understand how that's understandable, it's likely that you haven't been in that situation before and I encourage you to listen, rather than criticize. I used to be critical whenever I heard about a sexual assault survivor who didn't go to the authorities. (When something like that happens, you're supposed to go to the hospital or call the police, right?) But after talking to and e-mailing with thousands of people who have been assaulted, I fucking get it. And if you don't get it, cool, but remember *this is not about you.*

Here are a few courses of action you can take if you decide you want to report a rape or sexual assault, along with some facts you may not know:

* First and foremost, physically get yourself to a place where you feel like you're out of harm's way, whether that's your home or the home of a friend or family member.

* Call or walk into the nearest hospital. If you have no idea where you are, or feel as though you're currently in danger, call 911 (assuming there is a phone nearby). It's likely the hospital or police station will have someone trained to handle sexual assault cases. If for any reason you feel like the person you're dealing with isn't equipped to help you, ask to speak with the supervisor.

* If a hospital is the first place you go, they will ask if you wish to report what happened. Unless you are a minor, you are not legally obligated to report. If you'd like to do so, the hospital staff will connect you with local law enforcement.

* Filing a report with a police officer is just that: a report. You can decide whether or not you would like to press charges. The decision to press criminal charges against the rapist is unfortunately in the hands of the state you live in. It could be determined that there is not enough evidence. However, it's important to point out that filing an official report potentially could be evidence used years down the road should that person sexually assault someone again (odds are high they will). If multiple people file a police report alleging the same person raped them, that could be enough to take a case to court. The percentage of rapists who actually see a day in jail is low. Like . . . depressingly low. As in, six out of a thousand low.* This is why filing a report is important.

* If no criminal suit is brought, you have the option to file a civil suit. Unfortunately, the only good outcome for this would be monetary compensation.

* Some (few) sexual assault cases result in a plea bargain, which means that the perpetrator agrees to plead guilty in exchange for a lighter sentence or penalty. The plus side to this is that the victim isn't required to testify.

* Speaking of evidence, the best form of it can be taken with a rape kit, administered by a member of the hospital staff. It's extremely important that you avoid showering and going to the bathroom if at all possible. Stay in whatever clothes you're wearing, and don't touch your hair. This will give you the best shot at having the necessary evidence collected for a conviction. Every state has a different set of guidelines, but here are items typically found in a rape kit:

---

* "The Criminal Justice System: Statistics," website Rape, Abuse & Incest National Network, https://www.rainn.org/statistics/criminal-justice-system.

— a comb

— bags for evidence (your clothes, hair, DNA samples, etc.)

— supplies for taking and storing blood samples

* If you wish to have a rape kit done, it can take up to four hours. You might have photos taken of your body if there are marks on you, which will feel invasive as fuck but it also may help send a rapist to jail. If you go into panic mode and can't continue with the exam, that's okay. Tell the nursing staff. If you do continue, the rape kit will be sent away for testing. You may have the unfortunate experience of being in a city that has a rape kit backlog, which means there are years of kits sitting on shelves, waiting to be tested (and you thought the DMV was horrific).

* In addition to DNA samples and photographs, you'll be asked about your medical and sexual history. These questions will help investigators form a timeline of events so they can accurately evaluate the DNA results.

* You'll also go through a medical examination of your entire body, including every crevice and orifice, done by a trained professional. They'll be looking for cuts as well as any possible DNA on your body left by the perpetrator.

* The hospital should offer you an STI screening and a pregnancy test if you are a woman who was raped by a man. If they don't, ask for them.

See the resources section (page 235) for organizations that might be helpful if you know or suspect you've been sexually assaulted.

CONCLUSION

Final Thoughts

Time for the big closer!

While we sincerely wish we could end this book by giving everyone a mind-blowing orgasm, we honestly just don't have that in us. But we can summarize some take-homes for you to hold in your heart always and forever:

* Become familiar with your flaws and actively work to fix them (that way you get to call yourself out before others do!).

* Have a sense of humor, especially toward the dark shit. Your mom died. You got fired from your dream job. Your boyfriend dumped you after he banged your sister. We *promise* you that you can laugh at that. It may take a sec, but you'll get there.

* Enjoy sex, and don't be afraid to place importance on sexual compatibility in your relationship. Best friends who don't fuck are just really good partners—you can enjoy spending time with him/her/them, but don't get excited to touch their genitals if you're not compatible. That person is your best friend, not your soulmate.

* Appreciate your body—it houses your soul. If you don't, figure out the steps you need to take to get there. Your body is your packaging. You have to see it every day so you might as well like it.

* Try new stuff. Sexual stuff. Unless it absolutely appalls you or involves people or things you know you're not emotionally ready for—and may never be—you might surprise yourself and find that having icing licked off your clit is even more satisfying than licking icing off a cake.

* Always keep in mind that another person's success or good looks or sex drive or income is not a reflection of what you lack. It's easy to forget, considering there are entire industries that profit off making you feel like an unfuckable piece of garbage. Fear and shame are merely control tactics. Organic facial serum and six pack abs don't make you sexy. Being yourself, freely and unapologetically, makes you sexy, and bonus: it's free as fuck!

* Be a good listener. Blindly shouting opinions on your social media platforms or screaming at a woman walking into a clinic does not yield progress, it just fuels selfish rage. Listen to the people you disagree with. Listen to your sexual partner. Listen to your kids. Having a voice is important, but it's amazing how much you can learn by shutting the hell up every once in a while.

* Vote.

* Love yourself; it's easier than you think. You're like, pretty cool.

We know you're a queen and you're fierce, and you've said bye to Felicia, and you're not a basic bitch, and you're independent AF, and you're not about to deal with any fuck bois, but after reading this book, how well do you really know you?

Pop Quiz! Fill in the blanks.

1. My greatest source of shame is _____.

2. This shame is not real because _____.

3. _____ is someone in my life who takes away from my happiness rather than adding to it.

4. A sexual fantasy I have that I've never discussed with a significant other is _____.

5. The most important thing in my quest for sexual freedom is:
_____

6. I would like to stop obsessing so much over this part of my body:
_____

7. The best quality I can bring to my life is _____.

8. The best quality I can bring to someone else's life is _____.

9. My ideal partner is many things, but most of all they are:
_____

10. I hate my _____, but I promise to work on loving it.

11. I am sorry for saying/thinking this about a fellow woman:
_____

_____

12. I love myself, but something I can do to start loving myself more is
_____

13. My _____ (something non-aesthetic) makes me beautiful.

14. The sexiest part of my body is my _____ (something aesthetic).

15. Being attractive is nice, and I should not shit on women who are attractive merely because they are attractive, but something more important to me than physical beauty is _____.

16. The last person I fucked would say this about me:
_____

Krystyna

Wow, we did it you guys! Corinne and I wrote a book. You *read* a book. We're killing it! I never in a million years thought that my life would be so beautifully whacky and fulfilling, but that's what happens when you dream big and work hard. I hope you do the same in whatever path excites you the most. I hope this book has given you a new perspective or, at the very least, the reassurance that no matter what life throws your way, you are not alone. Sexual intercourse is how we all got here in the first place, so let's remind ourselves as often as possible to enjoy our sexuality and respect the sexuality of others. Sex is such a beautiful part of being human and if we all stopped worrying about what everyone else thinks and focused on honestly communicating how we feel and what we want, the world would be a better place. Repressing a part of yourself *never* ends well. Never sell yourself short. You matter and you are loved, even if you don't always feel that way. Be yourself, have fun, and for the love of Beyoncé, vote in your local and general elections. I love you all.

Corinne

Recording a sex-themed podcast for the past almost four years has been silly, sad, frustrating, exhausting, infuriating, educational, and rewarding. You may have noticed I didn't say sexy. If there's anything I've learned from *Guys We Fucked,* it's that there's so much more to sex than being sexy. And while sex really should be added to Maslow's hierarchy, it's not everything. At the start of this whole thing, sex and relationships with men were damn near killing me, and now they're simply complementing this really great life I created while I was taking a break from all that. Don't get me wrong, I'm still miserable, but at least that misery has nothing to do with a man.

Abortion and Sexual Assault Resources

Abortion Resources

WOMEN ON WAVES

www.womenonwaves.org

If you live in a country where abortion is illegal, you still have options. Local laws do not apply in international waters, which are twelve miles off the coast of any country. Women on Waves wants to stop unsafe abortions and empower women by giving them the freedom of choice. They send out boats filled with professionals who can provide training, information, contraceptive pills, workshops, and safe and legal abortion services.

WOMEN ON WEB

www.womenonweb.org

If you live in a country where you have no access to a safe abortion, are less than ten weeks pregnant, and have no severe illnesses, this website will refer you to a licensed doctor who can give you a medical consultation and provide you with safe abortion pills to administer at home. There is an informative Q&A section as well as stories and photos from women who have used their services, which we highly recommend reading.

THE NATIONAL NETWORK OF ABORTION FUNDS
https://abortionfunds.org

This network's vision, as stated on their website, is "a world where every reproductive decision, including abortion, takes place in thriving communities that are safe, peaceful, and affordable. We envision a world where all people have the power and resources to care for and affirm their bodies, identities, and health for themselves and their families—in all areas of their lives. As we shift the conversation about abortion, it will become a real option, accessible without shame or judgment." They provide access to information and financial resources for low-income women to receive the care and knowledge they need.

REPRODUCTIVE HEALTH ACCESS PROJECT
www.reproductiveaccess.org

This organization publishes research on abortion care, in hopes of highlighting its inaccessibility. They assist doctors who want the training to provide abortion services, and they offer clinics and doctors accurate educational materials for their patients.

Sexual Assault Resources

THE NATIONAL SEXUAL ASSAULT HOTLINE
1-800-656-HOPE (4673)

This number will connect you with a local professional who can help you find where to report a rape and/or guide you to mental health counseling. The hotline was created and is operated by RAINN (Rape, Assault, and Incest National Network). They have a state law database on their website (https://apps.rainn.org/policy) where you can enter your zip code and learn about any laws in your area having to do with sexual assault and reporting, since there is a statute of limitations on sexual assault, meaning that you only have a certain number of years to report the crime.

SAFE HORIZON
www.safehorizon.org
1-800-621-HOPE (4673)

This organization contains resources for victims of rape, child abuse, domestic violence, stalking, and youth homelessness. Whether you need to be connected with legal representation or you need someone to tell you how to report sexual assault, they will make sure you have all the information needed and are connected with the right people to help you.

Krystyna

Krystyna's Acknowledgments

This book would not be possible without all of the lovely humans around the globe who listen to *Guys We Fucked*. To everyone who has ever e-mailed us, thank you for trusting Corinne and I with your secrets, insecurities, and current life kerfuffles. You've given us a unique window into what it means to be human, and reading your e-mails makes me feel more connected to the world in a way I never thought possible. To my parents, I cannot thank you enough for raising me with kindness, patience, and a sense of humor. I am honored to be your daughter and I love you both so much. To DJ, I'm so glad that you're my brother; I wouldn't have survived the past twenty-nine years without you. Seeing you become a father has been a joy I can't fully articulate in words. Melissa, thank you for making my life better. Our friendship means everything to me. You are a superhero who improves the lives of children and families on a daily basis, and I'm constantly in awe of you. To Daria, Ashley, and Stephanie, thank you for keeping me sane throughout the past ten years. We've come a long way since trying to sneak our nineteen-year-old asses into night clubs! To Michele, Claire, and Liz, you are three remarkable, beautiful souls, thank you for inspiring me since high school. To Wendi, you are one of the most talented stand-up comedians I've ever met. We're so great and talented and awesome! To Chef Jeff, our friendship means so much to me, and you are the best chef in all the land. To Corinne, you are the best comedy wife a gal could ask for. This career journey (lol) is so fucking weird and there isn't another human on the planet I'd rather experience it with. To Rick, thank you for all of your encouragement and pushing me to be the best comedian I can be. To Stephen, I will always remember you as one of the great loves of my life. Thank you for all that you have taught me about love, life, and myself.

CORINNE

Corinne's Acknowledgments

I want to thank my mom for being a stupendous example of a woman; my dad for instilling in me the love of telling a funny story; my brother for keeping me mildly humble; Tommy for making me feel like I am also getting a Ph.D. in sexual psychology without doing any of the work and also for being the only one I'm sure will get the dozen Alanis references I make in this book; Paula for putting up with a self-obsessed best friend and being my sister in cuntiness since middle school; James for being confident enough to date the cohost of the *Guys We Fucked* podcast, for being unapologetically yourself, and for picking the smart, funny girl (you have great taste); Sir Alfred Hitchcock for being a good boy and introducing me to a new level of love; Anthony for helping us to write the book we wanted to write and for being a genuine fan; Hilary for stalking our asses for years and making my dreams come true—you're persistent like Geri Halliwell, girl; Sydney for your encouragement and hours of hard work; Kris for being the voice of reason in this completely unreasonable business and also the classiest motherfucker I know; Frank for breaking my heart (sincerely); Alanis Morissette for getting me through that heartbreak (and all the others); stand-up comedy for keeping me sane; all the guys I've fucked for really bringing it; the #FUCKERS for being so loyal and for keeping this conversation going; and to all the little girls who are reading this, never doubt that you are valuable and powerful and deserving of every chance and opportunity in the world to pursue and achieve your own dreams. Okay, yes, I did steal that last part from Hillary Clinton. But while we're here, I wanna thank her too.

BONUS CHAPTER

Breakups: An Update

Corinne

Since writing this book, I have decided to end my relationship with James. I still love him. I still think about him. I still care about his well-being (please stop smoking). I still like his Instagram photos. I still call him after a bad show. I still feel like we share a connection that is deeper than any relationship—both romantic and non-romantic—I've had before.

This is a position I have never been in, and a different level of hard. With Panera, I was informed my relationship was ending. With boyfriends before that, I no longer felt intertwined with them, in love with them, or that we had any more growing to do together. With James, I had to decide, like Mary Poppins, that I had done all I could do, given all I could give, and it was time to fly off with my umbrella to a new project. While I believed, and believe, James is a kindred spirit, I felt very alone in the relationship toward the end and gave up on it before it was over because I realized, like so many things in my life, the relationship was no longer serving me.

I don't think of men as projects going into relationships. I certainly don't seek messes that I can eagerly clean up or charity work I can do in the form of a human, but I continually find myself giving all that

I have until I am merely a stump to sit on like the tree in Shel Silverstein's beautiful children's book.

I am devastated, but this time around it's a functioning devastated. I haven't cried very much, I'm eating, I'm laughing, I'm hanging out with friends, I'm drinking, and it's ending well. I'm okay It's nice to be devastated and okay, to feel a void but have it not stop me in my tracks. I was not looking to be single, I was not unhappy being in a relationship, but I was unhappy being in *that* relationship. I was tired of competing with a phone screen or a news story or a political ideology for attention. I was tired of having to remind someone to love me.

Shortly before I decided to end things with James, Krystyna and I had a conversation during which we stopped to think of a real-life example of a heterosexual relationship in which the woman was getting more support than, or even an equal amount of support as, the man. We couldn't think of one.

Cohosting the podcast, people are constantly coming to us with their problems and asking us for advice. As of late, it often feels like perhaps there is no room for our own problems any longer. After all, we have been given this wonderful opportunity, and to spend time on our own issues would be to take away time that could lend a chance at salvation to someone else.

I feel like I give out empowering, thoughtful, and good advice. Advice that will make peoples' lives better and encourage them to make stronger choices. I started asking myself, "When will I give myself the gift of taking my own advice?"

This past spring, I gave myself a very belated present, and for the first time in perhaps forever, took some of the relationship advice I have bereaved myself of for so long. For I knew to salvage the relationship I had nurtured for four years with my single self, I would have to let the one with James go. And so, I did. Because I've loved James for two years, but I've loved myself forever.

And that is where I'll leave it. Because if working on this book has taught me anything, it's that I have more important things to do than write about men.

Krystyna

In an effort to get my joy back and finally become a well-functioning adult, I ended my relationship with Stephen. I'm sharing these details with you because this breakup was the hardest decision I've had to make thus far in my life, and it is more than worthy of its own bonus chapter in this book, which I hope is helping you navigate the world a bit better.

So, what happened? Well, I'm going skip over the specific qualities about Stephen that ultimately led me to end the relationship because I'm *finally* learning the value of keeping certain details private. Parts of who he is played a factor, but it was mostly realizing what I needed to do for *myself*. I want to pause here, because I'm sure you've heard people say this before: "I needed to do it for myself." My comfort zone over the past few years has been to *always* put someone else's needs before my own, and, for the past seven years, that "someone else" was Stephen. Maybe this could have been sustainable; however, recently I've been catapulted so far beyond my comfort zone in so many areas of my life that I suddenly realized I was metaphorically rolling around naked in a field of broken glass, and something had to change.

As I've mentioned many times in this book and on the podcast, the desire to sleep with other people had been floating in my head for a few years, but I never felt compelled to act on it. My brain had always been in too chaotic of a place to make a life-changing decision. My mind was swarming with thoughts of the heartache I'd have to endure without Stephen, the anxiety over the possibility that I would be making a huge mistake by ending things with him, and the fear of being alone and sitting with that deep sadness. I was afraid that that sadness would engulf my entire body and eat me alive.

Luckily, although my brain was not capable of making the decision to sleep with someone else . . . my vagina was. Listen, I wouldn't normally recommend cheating on someone, but I ended up sleeping with another guy the night before I broke up with Stephen, and it was exactly the push I needed. Part of me feels like I should say how terrible and guilty I felt because cheating is not something "good" people do, but that would be a load of bullshit. I desperately needed that push. I needed to know that my vagina wasn't dead and that I was still capable of having the sexual appetite I once knew and loved, which I felt slowly fading during the final year Stephen and I were together. I was so relieved to realize that that part of me had not died, it was just lying dormant because I was in a relationship that no longer served me emotionally or sexually. It's comforting to know that when my brain is in too chaotic of a state to make such a mind-altering decision, my body can step up to the plate.

I left this guy's apartment that night feeling this overwhelming excitement over rekindling my sexuality. I had been suppressing that part of me because the thought of living my life without Stephen felt like jumping off a cliff. Before this night, I had consulted with friends and family on what the fuck I should do. They all agreed very quickly, almost too quickly, that I had outgrown the relationship. If you can't decide whether it's a good idea to leave someone, I suggest confiding in friends and family members who know you both well and whose opinions you respect and trust. That isn't to say you should do exactly what they suggest; you still need to listen to your gut and remember that it's ultimately your decision. I'm just saying, if every single person you talk to is telling you to get the fuck out, it's probably something you should consider.

The guy I fucked that night I would end up fucking for two more months. Not only did we have sex, we sexted, we exchanged naked photos and audio recordings of us talking dirty to each other, we had phone sex, and one night I bought two shower curtain liners and laid them on my bed so we could cover each other in lube and roll around naked. It was very fun.

And then this new guy broke things off. And for the first time since the day I met Stephen, I was truly alone. I sat in my apartment for weeks, and I cried and screamed and drooled and curled up in the fetal position wanting to die. I felt that sadness I was so afraid of, and I couldn't have imagined it would be so painful. And *this* is where all that hard work you've been meaning to do on yourself but keep putting off starts to happen. Existing in this concerning state of mind and really *being* with your feelings is the first step toward personal growth after breaking up with your long-term partner. If you've been there, you know exactly what I'm talking about. If you haven't, but you're desperately clinging to someone or something in order to avoid feeling your feelings, I challenge you to stop clutching that Band-Aid for dear life. I have a strong hunch that your world will open up in ways you never thought possible. You'll be surprised by how resilient you actually are.

Index

shaming, 58–65, 81, 203. *See also specific types of sex*

sex ed, 89, 201–4

sexual acts, 101–41; anal sex, 110–19; laws and, 140–41; masturbation, 103–9; period sex, 128–29; rape fantasies and, 135–39; sending nude photos, 130–32; three-ways, 120–27

sexual assault, 5, 26, 48–49, 50, 200, 204, 221–27; resources, 235–40; what to do, 224–27

sexually transmitted infections (STIs), 40, 91, 129, 153–54, 202, 203, 227

shame, 5–6, 21, 28, 29–85, 97–99, 138; anal sex, 116; fart-, 169–70; femasculation, 71–81; historical roots of, 34–35; introduction to, 31–33; male emotions and, 82–85; masturbation, 106; one-night stands, 52–57; parents and, 42–51; religion and, 36–38; self-love and, 66–70; sisterhood and, 59–62, 81; slut-shaming, 58–65, 81, 203; social media and, 35; sources of, 42–51; strong-shaming, 62–65

Shpancer, Noam, 40

Simmons, Gene, 146

sisterhood, 59–62, 81; Ten Commandments, 61–62

slavery, 38

slut-shaming, 58–65, 81, 203

smartphones, 35, 175, 217; sending nude photos, 130–32

snooping, 173–76

social media, 35, 48, 54, 60, 68, 82, 162, 174, 175, 185, 186, 187, 193; shame and, 35; stalking, 185–88

Sorry About Last Night…, 4, 21

sperm, 40

stalking, 5; the ex, 185–88

Stand Up NY Labs, 5

Steinem, Gloria, 7

stress, 39, 92, 109

strong-shaming, 62–65

sugar, 92

suicide, 5, 27, 35; increase in, 35

Supreme Court, U.S., 212–13

TED Talks, 47, 162

television, 34, 37, 47, 75, 98, 168

terrorism, 82–83

testing, 153–54

three-ways, 120–27, 161; jealousy and, 125–27; wobbly-H, 134

Thrinder, 122

Tissot, Samuel-Auguste-David, 104

TRAP laws, 208–9, 213

Trump, Donald, 140, 163, 212, 213, 224

Twitter, 35, 54, 169, 187, 193

Upton, Kate, 73

urethra, 92, 93, 117

urinary tract infections (UTIs), 92–93

urination, 92

vagina, 9, 39–40, 89–93, 179; basics, 89–91; dryness, 215; insecurity, 97–99; muscles, 39; orgasm and, 93; sending nude photos, 130–32; type of labia, 89–91, 97; yeast infection, 91–92

vibrator, 126, 179

Village Voice, The, 76

violence, 5, 82–83

virginity, 15; loss of, 42–46

water, 220, 221

witchcraft, 34, 35

wobbly H, 134

woman-on-woman hatred, 59–62, 81

yeast infections, 91–92

Zen, 164

About the Authors

CORINNE FISHER is a stand-up comedian, writer, director, and actor originally from Union, NJ. She first made a splash with her debut one-woman show *Corinne Fisher: I Stalk You* (Dir. David Crabb), which had a highly attended run at The Peoples Improv Theater (The PIT) in the Summer of 2010 and was featured in *Time Out New York*. Since then, she has become a nationally recognized comedy headliner and has been invited to perform at multiple festivals, including the prestigious Just For Laughs Comedy Festival in Montreal, Moontower Comedy Festival in Austin, and the Boston Comedy Festival, as well at The Afghan Women's Writing Project series with SNL alum Rachel Dratch. On YouTube, she is the messed-up mind behind Internet vlogger Gina Sprinkles and the voice of Toiba on the cartoon web series *Mystery Squad Gals*, the brainchild of Ryan Duff. In print, she has penned multiple pieces for *Glamour* magazine. Corinne made her stand-up television debut in 2014 on the special "Under 30" episode of FOX's *Laughs*. She also cohosts a popular show at New York Comedy Club called *Nacho Bitches* with Blair Socci (from MTV's *Ladylike*). In the Summer of 2015, Corinne and fellow comic Katie Hannigan created *The Comedienne Project* (Dir. Ted Alexandro), a show challenging its participants to write and perform twenty new minutes of stand-up sans sex, dating, or relationship material, which was accepted into the NYC Fringe Festival and is now a monthly show at The Standing Room. Recently, Corinne started *Undie Party* with Boris Khaykin and Justin Perez, a floating comedy show sponsored by MeUndies with all proceeds going to New Alternatives for at-risk LGBTQ youth. Corinne holds a BFA in Film Direction from SVA and is proud that her first on-screen credit was for Michael Moore's *Sicko*. In her mind, she's best known for creating *Wannabe Weekly*, the online zine dedicated to the Spice Girls that lit up the Internet for five very special years in the late '90s/early '00s.

🐦 @PhilanthropyGal 📷 philanthropygal

🌐 CorinneFisher.com 📘 CorinneFisherComedy t thephilanthropygirl

KRYSTYNA HUTCHINSON is a writer, stand-up comedian, and actress originally from Doylestown, Pennsylvania. After winning first place in both the International Thespian Festival monologue competition and the Philadelphia Shakespeare Competition her senior year of high school (two credits she will probably brag about until the day she dies), Krystyna attended Penn State University as a theater major. In an effort to actualize her dream of being on *Saturday Night Live*, she transferred to Marymount Manhattan College in the hopes of landing an internship at the show. Three years and two failed interviews later, Krystyna landed the internship and didn't kill herself. On her final day, she asked a writer for advice on getting an audition, to which he replied, "I don't know. Do stand-up, I guess?" So began Krystyna's stand-up career. While pursing stand-up, she joined forces with fellow comedian Corinne Fisher and created "Sorry About Last Night...." Together, the girls produced several hit stand-up shows, made a rap video, and performed in lots of bars, sushi restaurants, movie theaters, and outdoor tents. Three years into comedy duo-dom, the girls created *Guys We Fucked: The Anti Slut-Shaming Podcast* in which Corinne, dealing with the baggage of a bad break-up, and Krystyna, dealing with the baggage of following a porn star, interviewed the guys they fucked. The podcast quickly received praise from *The Daily Beast, Vogue, The Huffington Post, Mother Jones,* and CNN, as well as an opportunity to give a TEDx talk on sexuality and self-worth. Krystyna has written for *Splitsider, Glamour,* and, most recently, this very book. She's appeared on TV shows such as *Master of None* on Netflix and Comedy Central's *This Is Not Happening,* and she cohosts the hit monthly variety show *Glamourpuss* alongside comedian Wendi Starling at the legendary jazz venue Zinc Bar. When she isn't performing, writing, or chronically over-sharing intimate details on the podcast, odds are she's watching a Beyoncé music video on YouTube.

🐦 @KrystynaHutch 📷 krystynahutch

🌐 KrystynaHutchinson.com 📘 KrystynaHutchinson